Pastors, Chiefs, and Warlords

Pastors, Chiefs, and Warlords

THE MINISTRY OF BEING WITH

Bob Walters
with Kate Koppy

Foreword by Taylor Walters Denyer

RESOURCE *Publications* · Eugene, Oregon

PASTORS, CHIEFS, AND WARLORDS
The Ministry of Being With

Copyright © 2022 Bob Walters and Kate Koppy. All rights reserved. Except for brief quotations in critical publications or reviews, no part of this book may be reproduced in any manner without prior written permission from the publisher. Write: Permissions, Wipf and Stock Publishers, 199 W. 8th Ave., Suite 3, Eugene, OR 97401.

Resource Publications
An Imprint of Wipf and Stock Publishers
199 W. 8th Ave., Suite 3
Eugene, OR 97401

www.wipfandstock.com

PAPERBACK ISBN: 978-1-6667-3795-0
HARDCOVER ISBN: 978-1-6667-9812-8
EBOOK ISBN: 978-1-6667-9813-5

MARCH 15, 2022 12:40 PM

Contents

About this Book | ix

Foreword by Taylor Walters Denyer | xi

Introduction by Kate Koppy | xv

Heart of Darkness, Revisited | 1

Pastors, Chiefs, and Warlords
The Second Tour, the Preliminary Stages

Home in Indiana | 7
New York | 11
London to Kitwe | 14
Tenke | 18
Church Visits around Tenke | 23
Carrying the Robe and Collar | 28

Pastors, Chiefs, and Warlords
The Second Tour

Fungarume | 33
Kyubo | 35
Kasengeshi | 37
Mitwaba | 39
From Bicycles to a Boat | 41
The Boat Arrives | 43
Arrested in Malemba | 46
Trying to Explain the Mission of Friendly Planet Missiology | 50
To Kabalo | 54
The Snake House | 57
Kabumbulu | 59
Arrival in Kabalo | 62
Jackie | 65
Faith, Comfort, and Friendship | 67
Preaching in Kabalo | 70
Cycling around Kabalo | 73
Foyer | 74
Nvwendee's Village | 76
Return by Land Cruiser | 81
Visit of Dr. Ivan, the Congressman | 83
A List | 87
Fondo d'Congo | 88

On the River
The Third Tour

Going the Other Way | 93
Kansenia Gar, Remembered | 96
Kansenia to Lubudi, 2012 | 101
Zambikes | 105
Lubudi to Luena | 106
Luena to Bukama | 108
We're off to See the Bishop | 110
A Meeting at the Guest House | 116
Church Tours in and around Kamina | 118
Around Kamina | 121
Kabando Dianda and Nyembo Umpungu | 123
Kyungu wa Ngoy Bertin | 125
Kasanga | 127
Reading *War and Peace* | 131
Mulongo to Manono | 133
Entering the Manono District | 136
Manono | 138
Mission and Abandonment | 142
Three Water Projects | 144
Breaking Rules to Connect to the Past | 146
Manono to Kanteba | 148
Ride Back from Manono | 152
One More District | 156
Ashamed of the UMC | 161
The DS's School | 162
Truly Done | 164

Further Reading and Resources | 167

About this Book

THIS BOOK PICKS UP where Bob Walters' first book, *The Last Missionary*, left off. As with any sequel, the setting is the same, and many of the people who appeared on the pages of the first book show up here again. Unlike a sequel, this book stands on its own and can be read independently of the earlier book.

This is Bob's book, but it's not the book Bob would have written. When he died suddenly in July of 2017, Bob and I had just begun collaborating on this book. With the permission of Bob's wife, Teri, and their children, Taylor and Robbie, I continued working on the manuscript, supplementing with passages from and fact-checking against Bob's journals. I feel confident that what I present to you here is an accurate account of the Friendly Planet teams' trips in 2011 and 2012. What is missing and what I, as an editor, cannot provide are the additional conclusions and lessons that would have come from Bob having spent time revising with me.

While working on *The Last Missionary*, Bob and I fell into a repetitive pattern where I would point out an unfinished thought, and Bob would remind me that readers are supposed to think for themselves. I would tell him that I was a reader who had no idea what to think at that moment, and he would come back several days later with some more phrases or a few sentences that added more context or pointed toward his conclusion.

Because further conversation with Bob was unavailable, Taylor and I have brought more voices into the book you hold in your hands. Three of the Congolese colleagues who were part of these trips have contributed essays about their experiences, Taylor has written a foreword that contextualizes Friendly Planet's work, and I have offered an introduction about these bicycle trips as a devotional practice. We hope you enjoy the conversation and that you carry it further from this book into your communities of faith and service.

About this Book

As we were working during the white supremacist violence and anti-racist protests of 2019 and 2020 in the United States, Taylor and I wondered if the world needed another book in which a white man wrote about his experience in the Global South. A conversation with Joseph Mulongo, one of Bob's Congolese colleagues, allayed our misgivings. Joseph said:

> This book is written by an American who had the time to go into the mission field. This book will help Americans to understand our vision of mission: that if we want to go in mission, we must know people correctly. When we do not know people correctly, we want to do good, but we do things badly. This book helps Americans to understand how today's mission may be.
>
> The way of doing mission, Bob's way of understanding mission, has helped me, too. I have learned more working together. Marching with Bob, I have learned so many things. We need a new approach of mission. I don't hate or blame what the first missionaries have done. I do appreciate them and am very grateful. They did a great job, but there are so many things we need to fix.
>
> Reading this book can help not only Americans, but even Congolese, even my people, to fix some things if we want to do mission correctly.

Joseph's statement concurs with the overwhelming response we heard from the publication of *The Last Missionary*. This book can help us all do better by modeling the kind of intentional relationship we should cultivate in mission partnerships. For the Americans, as Bob relates here, this means surrendering the ego of leadership and learning to listen.

—Kate Koppy,
editor

Foreword

BUILT UPON AN EXISTING FOUNDATION of faithful cross-contextual friendships, Friendly Planet Missiology (FPM) was launched in 2009 to model a healthier alternative to the dominant mission model of the church in the USA, which relies on checkbooks, shipping containers, and poverty tourism. Our methods were initially incomprehensible to friends both stateside and in Congo. Why spend months traveling by bicycle and riverboat through a smoldering war zone? What would such a dangerous act accomplish? Trying to raise funds for these ventures proved nearly impossible, but Bob Walters was determined. And so, Joseph Mulongo, Daniel Mumba, Shabana Banza, Ngoy wa Kasongo (aka Éléphant), and others resolved that they would go with him.

On the Red Road, our team slowly began to find the words to articulate the theological grounding and pragmatic wisdom of these itinerant visitations to communities whose leaders were working amid exhaustion, grief, and institutional abandonment. We engaged in the kind of transformational conversations that can only happen in the liminal space of being "on the way" together. In the process, we came to understand the importance that journeying played in the formation of Jesus' first disciples and the early church.

The 2009 ride described in Bob's first book, *The Last Missionary*, soon gave birth to other FPM journeys, including a women's boat trip (led by Mary Kabamba), three youth/young adult rides, and the two rides found in this book. While FPM's numbers grew, we continued operating on a shoestring budget, proudly embracing the motto "small footprint; big change." Yes, over time, the friendships built on the road resulted in funds raised to support several locally-led initiatives: from the construction of a nursing school and women's training center to the sponsoring of scouting jamborees. But we understood that these initiatives had such a high success rate *because* of the solid relational foundation the FPM journeys created.

The book you are holding in your hands today was intended to be the second in a three-part series of FPM publications. Bob's idea was that his two books would constitute the first two parts and present the reader with what he had learned through his experiences. The third part would be my dissertation, *Decolonizing Mission Partnerships: Evolving Collaboration Between United Methodists in North Katanga and the United States of America*,[1] which would provide the academic framework. His unexpected death in 2017 reversed their publication dates, but it remains best to read the three books side by side.

Four additional books I strongly suggest adding to this reading list are Samuel Wells' *A Nazareth Manifesto: Being with God* (2015), Dana Robert's *Faithful Friendships* (2019), Ibram X. Kendi's *How to be an Anti-Racist* (2019), and Albert Memmi's 1957 classic *The Colonizer and the Colonized*, which remains sadly relevant even today. Read together, these works name and point to truths essential to understand for anyone attempting to form healthy cross-contextual relationships. They point to the toxic systems that we are all trapped within, our yearning and need for connection, and our mandate to be proactive in dismantling oppressive systems while recognizing that we will continue to make mistakes and learn from them.

No one was more aware than Bob himself of the contradictions he represented. He was a white male missionary heavily influenced by colonial romantic writings and the *National Geographic* photos of his youth. Nevertheless, he knew that the sooner the age of (neo)colonial missionaries ended, the better. He also knew that he could taste atonement through what he was doing with his friends in Congo.

Through their bicycle journeys together, Bob and Joseph Mulongo became not just collaborators but brothers. I functioned as the Type A in the trio, remotely monitoring their adventures like, as Bob enjoyed remarking, M in a James Bond novel. Together we could accomplish what we could not do alone. We—and the entire FPM family—became a "we" so much so that whenever Bob uses the word "we" in this book, more often than not, he does not mean "we Americans" but instead "we the Church in Congo."

As a closing note, I am happy to say that some of the assertions/critiques Bob made about the UMC's top leadership when he was writing this

---

1. Selected in 2019 for publication in the American Society of Missiology's Monograph Series.

Foreword

manuscript in 2017 are less accurate now than they were then. Views and behaviors are changing, and FPM is proud to have played a role in this change.

Taylor Walters Denyer
President, Friendly Planet Missiology and
Bishop's Executive Assistant for Strategic Partnerships and Engagement,
The United Methodist Church's North Katanga Episcopal Area

Introduction

As I've worked with Bob to prepare both *The Last Missionary* and *Pastors, Chiefs, and Warlords: The Ministry of Being With* for publication, I've been struck by the way that these journeys were for him a sort of meditation.

In the twenty-first century in the United States, the word *meditation* is generally associated with images of stillness—sitting on the floor with legs folded together, eyes closed, hands resting on knees—and with images of quietness—the sound of the breath, soft music, or white noise. Such meditation is more likely found in a yoga class or a Buddhist temple than in a Christian church.

Christianity, however, has a long and varied tradition of "meditation that moves." These "moving meditations" include making a pilgrimage to local shrines and holy sites or to the distant Holy Land. In medieval literature and maps of Europe, these regional and international pilgrimage routes can be seen crisscrossing the landscape—from London to Canterbury, along the Camino de Santiago through France and Spain, from all parts of the Christian world to Jerusalem. Some of these routes are still in active use; some exist only as historical markers on modern roads, and some only as memories.

When a believer commits to a pilgrimage, the destination is the main point, and pilgrims are willing to sacrifice a lot—comfort, money, time—to reach that destination. But they also choose a meaningful path. Part of the discipline of pilgrimage is the departure from home. The pilgrim leaves their familiar space, the geography they know, their culture. The disorientation of the journey itself is part of the preparation for reaching the destination. The discipline of the pilgrimage is persistence through hardship, through aching muscles, through uncomfortable weather, through the unfamiliar. In the process, pilgrims report that they draw closer to God, learn about themselves, and finish the journey with a new perspective on their place in

Introduction

the world. However, the moving meditation of the pilgrimage path is not available to every believer.

In local cathedrals throughout the Christian world, labyrinths provide a way to pray on one's feet without traveling to a faraway place. Unlike a maze that challenges the user to find the one correct path to the goal among wrong turns and dead ends, a prayer labyrinth has only one path to the center and back. This single path, however, folds back on itself and wraps around the center. The discipline of meditation in a labyrinth is not to remain still and quiet but to follow the guidance of the path wherever it goes.

The center of the labyrinth is the destination, but the path is the point. Often the path moves further from the center before it arrives there. The complex paths of large labyrinths like those in the cathedral at Chartres (France) or in the National Cathedral (Washington, DC) feel deceptive. The path takes the user close to the center and then sends them back out to the edge multiple times before finally leading into the heart of the labyrinth. The labyrinth requires a certain discipline: keep moving and surrender to the path, even when it seems to be going away from the destination.

Those who have access may make walking this kind of labyrinth a regular part of their prayer life. Americans tend to value innovative things and things that help them make progress, and they can be surprised to find that walking the same path from entrance to center and back yields new insights each time. Some labyrinth users empty their minds as they walk, making space for insight to arrive. Others focus on a question or a dilemma as they walk, turning options around in their mind as their feet follow the path, hoping to leave the labyrinth with a new perspective.

The bicycle and boat journeys that the Friendly Planet Missiology team has taken through the Congo are both pilgrimage and labyrinth. Tours two and three, the journeys recounted in this book, follow some of the same highways and trails as the first tour in *The Last Missionary*; the team visits some of the same towns and talks to many of the same people. But as with the great cathedral labyrinths, the path is the point, not the destination. The Friendly Planet team embraces the discipline of sending its tires ever forward. While the journey is the point, each journey also has a destination. These destination sites have not been identified as shrines and consecrated by the church, Methodist or otherwise, but they are nonetheless holy.

When Bob and Joseph Mulongo started to plan their bicycle trip, the goal of the Friendly Planet team was to ride to Kabalo to visit Pastor Jackie.

Introduction

On their first ride in 2010, they were unable to make it to Kabalo and did not reach their goal. Their second journey in 2011, described in the first half of this book, covers the same ground as the 2010 trip and continues to their original goal in Kabalo. In revisiting familiar ground, Bob finds new insights.

On these pages, Bob guides readers through the reflections and ideas that came to him through his moving meditations. The reflections contributed by Bob's Congolese colleagues, Joseph Mulongo, Shabana Banza, and Jaqueline Ngoy Mwayuma, offer additional perspectives. At times the questions and insights shared are highly specific. The reader is invited to empathize with the Friendly Planet team's experiences connecting the United Methodist Church in the United States with one corner of the Global South.

Simultaneously, readers are challenged to see the interconnectedness of all things. The colonial structures of power that perpetuate inequality and exploitation in the North Katanga region of the Democratic Republic of the Congo are similar to those in other postcolonial spaces worldwide. The model of deep listening and support for projects driven by local leadership has the power to transform the way Christians around the world engage in mission partnerships with one another.

The end of this book shows Bob recognizing his own limits, ready to go home at the end of the 2012 tour. He would make more visits to Congo between this tour and his death in 2017, but no more 1000-kilometer bicycle rides. His sudden and unexpected death shocked his communities in Indiana and the Congo. We were all rocked back on our heels for a moment. But as we moved through our grief, we all, individually and collectively, resolved to continue the work we had been doing with him.

When I asked Joseph about the future of Friendly Planet Missiology's work in Congo, he picked up the paradoxical metaphor—the Last Missionary—Bob used for himself:

> Bob was the last missionary who lived like the Congolese. He is the last missionary who loved the North Katanga and Tanganyika people. He was doing his best to spend his time with people, to understand people's way of living, of understanding things. They called him Baba Bob everywhere. "Baba" is someone who gives his life for the sake of family, for his children. Bob took risks with his life for North Katanga. This was very special.
>
> In all the time I spent with Bob, it was not difficult to know if he was happy or not. His smile always showed it. And what people are still missing is Bob's smile. Bob was a good preacher, and his

Introduction

message is still missed. But I know because he started a work that is not achieved yet, that is still going on, God is providing other servants who are continuing Bob's work.

As I type this, I can picture Bob's smile, particularly his wry smile. He called himself the last missionary and dedicated his life to changing the way that mission looked so that the next generation of American and Congolese Christians could build better relationships.

This book is an invitation to join the pilgrimage and a call to walk the labyrinth.

Kate Koppy, ed.
Moscow, Russia
2021

Heart of Darkness, Revisited

*or, An Introduction to the Second Tour
On the Congo River, January 2011*

IN THE VILLAGES OF northeastern Katanga, life takes all day, and then some. When the sun sets, there is still a lot of living yet to finish before sleeping. Women's work begins at four in the morning and does not end until midnight. Fishermen go out on the water before dawn and do not return until it is too dark to fish. In the evenings, nets need mending. Farmers will often spend the night in their fields, which are too far from home for a daily commute. Life takes all day, and then some.

Nonetheless, it is a magical time when the sun goes down. The air cools a bit, and the pressure of a hard life relaxes just a bit. The moon and stars, augmented by a charcoal fire or maybe a battery-powered LED lantern, provide the necessary light. It is a time of children playing and laughing. It is the time when church choirs practice and families sing for their own entertainment. It is a time for old men to argue politics—loudly.

Our boat has no lights for night navigation on the river, so we've tied up along the shore and will sleep somewhere north of Ankora. With our bicycles, motorcycles, and gear, we are going down the Lualaba (the Congo River) on our riverboat, the *Indiana*. We won't move again until first light.

I'm spending this evening reading *Heart of Darkness* and imagining telling you this story. It's not the first time I've read *Heart of Darkness*, but a riverboat going down the Congo River is the perfect setting for reading the book. I note that we are one watershed over from where David Livingstone died—on the watershed where he wanted to be.

1

We're on our way from Mulongo to Kabalo to visit Pastor Jacqueline Ngoy Mwayuma, the District Superintendent of the Kabalo District. Our journey is the maiden voyage of the *Indiana* and the greatest adventure to date for the team we call Friendly Planet Missiology. Pastor Jackie serves a district that suffered greatly in the war in eastern Congo, and she was sent there to help rebuild the community. We're going to visit her to make sure she doesn't feel abandoned, and to open up a supply line.

The Friendly Planet team is led by the Rev. Joseph Mulongo, District Superintendent of the Mulongo District. This is the joke that never ends. He introduces himself, "I am Mulongo of Mulongo." The joke keeps getting better. There is also a Dr. Ivan Mulongo in our story, former director of the Mulongo Hospital in the village of Mulongo and current representative of the Malemba-Nkulu District in parliament.

The Rev. Daniel Mumba is the district superintendent of the Tenke District, where this tour began. Tenke is the home base for our team—safe and comfortable. There's no running water there, but Tenke does have electricity from the railroad station. Mumba's particular interest in this trip is visiting the Kabalo District, where he began his ministry but hasn't been since the war.

The Rev. Floribert Kora, Africa University graduate and lecturer at the Kamina Methodist University, comes along with us because of his experience in the war zone. He is one of the pastors who remained in their appointments as the war swept through their districts. He is also one of the pastors Bishop Ntambo sent to talk the warlords into coming to the peace table.

I'm the missionary. I'm the package—more a piece of cargo than a productive team member. None of us yet knows what my contribution will be.

Éléphant is the captain of the *Indiana*. His birth name is Ngoy wa Kasongo, but he carries the name Éléphant proudly. It is carved into his fishing pirogue. Mulongo says the nickname came from his soccer days: he was so rigid and strong that he never fell over when pushed. As a fisherman and a village elder, Éléphant also carries the appellation "chief." Éléphant has earned this unofficial title by taking available resources and growing them into a thriving fishing business. He's also an ace mechanic, having once been the driver for a British Brethren missionary. He owns two motorcycles, one of which he built from scraps. His strength, leadership, and mechanical know-how mean Éléphant was the logical choice to be our new boat's captain.

Éléphant has brought four others for his crew. They all wear the teal blue uniform t-shirts of Team Friendly Planet proudly. I've given Éléphant an Indianapolis Colts cap to wear for photos, but I think he prefers his own old orange baseball cap. Éléphant and I do not share a common language. He does not know much French and seldom speaks Swahili. His language is Kiluba, the language of the village. The only words I know in Kiluba are the handful he has taught me. Over the years, we've learned to communicate in other ways. We read each other's body language. This kind of communication without language doesn't always work. As action-oriented introverts, though, Éléphant and I have become good at this.

Besides the Friendly Planet Team, the *Indiana* is carrying a cargo of 110 sheets of metal roofing, which we will deliver to a clinic under construction in the village of Kabumbulu Kimbayo. The villages of Kabumbulu form the "Red Zone" of the Mai-Mai, the home of the warlord Nvwendee. Mulongo tells me, "Everything you have heard about the war, it happened here." I've heard a lot. But I'll tell you more about it when we get to Kabalo.

The *Indiana* is also carrying three passengers on this trip. Two—a man and a woman—are being returned home from hospital stays at the Garenganze, a British Brethren hospital in Mulongo. They are both very quiet and sleep most of the time. The third passenger is a woman who had begged Mulongo to take her back to her home in Kabalo to complete some family legal business. After telling her "no" three times, Mulongo relented. There was no expectation she'd contribute anything in exchange for the passage, but she jumped right in and took charge of the cooking. It is fascinating watching her kill, clean, and cook a chicken using river water and a small charcoal fire in the bow of the boat with no tools other than a pot and a big knife. She has been a real help.

The men take turns cooking, too—even Mulongo. Two or three of the crew seem to particularly enjoy the task. We have not made a duty roster, so people just seem to do what they have fun doing. Everyone knows their place in the social pecking order, but there is also a countering egalitarianism, where no task is beneath anyone. The duties of everyday life are simple and obvious—cooking, cleaning, serving—but they require everyone's effort. In the midst of our almost overwhelming struggles for subsistence, life together is still joy-filled. Not only am I having fun on this cruise down the Congo, but the whole crew is also enjoying it. Alongside our tasks, the team sings to fill the hours on the river. I occasionally recognize the tune of the song and can join in. "It is Well with My Soul," sung in Swahili, with feeling, by strong male voices in harmony, always brings me close to tears.

Mostly, though, I'm an observer. I spend this time on the river reflecting, writing in my journal, and imagining telling you these stories of the days on the river or of crossing the mountains on a bicycle. But mostly what I want to tell you is what I've learned from sitting in the villages. I have, of course, learned a lot about the tragedies of war and poverty, hunger and disease, but lots of people can tell you those stories. The more important thing I've learned, the most important stories I want to tell you are about the competence and strength of the leadership in the villages and remote districts of Katanga. The conventional wisdom remains that African leaders are too corrupt, too trapped in cultural norms, or too primitive and unsophisticated to understand complex issues. (I must add that these stereotypes are believed by Africans, as well as Americans and Europeans.) There is enough local leadership in the villages of the eastern Congo to solve the problems that plague them. For a time, it's necessary to move resources from parts of the world where there are abundant resources to places of great need. Nevertheless, there are more than adequate resources for rebuilding these war-torn communities right beneath their feet.

The message to you readers outside of the Congo is, "We've got to get some help to these people, and we've got to get it there right now." The message to the people of the villages is, "Everything you need, God has already provided." Both messages are true. The biblical text our team leads with from the second chapter of Revelation echoes this both-and message: "I know of your poverty and your suffering, but you are rich!"

I sit on the gunnel of the boat and marvel that so very few *wazungu* (white people) get to see what I am seeing. There's probably not another white person for 500 miles. To be this deeply immersed in the village life inside the war zone of eastern Congo is a rare, rare treat. And you should see this sunrise.

As we begin this journey, I think about how much has happened between the end of the first voyage and the start of this one. So, let me tell you about it.

Pastors, Chiefs, and Warlords

The Second Tour, the Preliminary Stages

Home in Indiana

1,000-mile ride, September 2010

IN JANUARY 2010, I rode my bicycle 1,000 miles around the North Katanga Conference of The United Methodist Church in the Democratic Republic of the Congo with my Congolese colleagues. It was an unprecedented undertaking for all of us. We learned a lot about ourselves, about working as a team, and about the villages we visited. *The Last Missionary*, my first book, tells the story of this bike ride. In this book, we pick up with my arrival home from that trip.

When I come back from extended time in the Congo, I go into a period of decompression. It is hard to estimate how deep I've been in the villages and in my own spirit. My mind is full of new ideas. But I can't let them burst out all at once. Like a SCUBA diver, I have to come up slowly.

The difficulties of the decompression are aggravated by jet lag: I fall asleep at 5:00 p.m. every day. On the good side, I'm up at 5:00 in the morning, raring to go.

This time, as with roughly half the times I've returned, I'm suffering from a fever. I hate to go to the doctor because a stateside doctor is clueless concerning tropical diseases. I could have malaria—I don't know. But neither do the doctors. And doctors in the States refuse to consider diagnosing malaria without a blood test. My missionary friends who have nearly died from malaria tell me that the blood test will often miss the little malaria bugger swimming in your blood. Going to the doctor feels like a waste of time, and I'm determined to ride out this fever. However, my wife

Teri persuades me that I need to have this sorted out before heading for Ft. Myers on her spring break, so I go.

The doctor won't even work with me and insists on sending me to a tropical disease specialist. Now I really regret going to the doctor. I hate the time wasted and the money thrown away on a test that will tell us nothing. And besides that, I'm sick with a fever and just want to go home and rest in comfort.

The diagnosis comes in—Baghdad Boils. This seems crazy. I did have a sore on my leg from the bite of a sand flea, the carrier of Baghdad Boils, and I had aggravated it to its angry state by over-scratching. But Baghdad Boils? I look it up. (Sure, with the internet, now everyone is an MD.) But Baghdad Boils is really rare. As the name suggests, the only cases have been among soldiers in the Iraq War, and the symptoms are a lot scarier than what I'm presenting. It might not be malaria, but malaria makes more sense than Baghdad Boils.

At the end of the day, I am given a prescription for antibiotics and sent on my way. Teri's question is, "Do we have to worry about going into the water with that ugly sore on his leg?"

Doctor: "No problem."

My question: "What about beer?"

Doctor: "No problem."

So, the doc prescribes antibiotics and a week drinking beer on the beach. I am completely satisfied with the outcome.

When I return, the real problem is that I'm not speaking. In my decompressing state, I am silent. You'd think that I would have a lot to say, a lot to tell. On the airplane ride home, my mind raced with all the stories and learnings that I had to share. But even with Teri, I can't talk. Especially with Teri, I can't talk.

It doesn't help that Teri considers it her right to be mad at me for abandoning her. By her count, she deserves at least a week, maybe two, of pissed-off anger. I can't say that she's wrong.

But I think that even aside from her anger, I still wouldn't be able to talk.

As with earlier returns, it has been months since I've spoken to anyone in English. Or, more accurately, it has been months since I've talked with anyone who understands English at the same level as I speak it. I know that I have not actually been speaking in other languages, but I have been listening hard to people speaking in other languages. I have spent months not speaking, just listening.

I wanted a rolling start at telling everyone what I had seen and heard and learned, but I have nothing to say.

We drive down to Ft. Myers Beach with friends and spend a week at a mom-and-pop vacation motel unit with a kitchen. It's nothing fancy, but it's right on the beach, and therefore, perfect. We spend the days walking in the sand and reading. For fun beach reading, I love Carl Hiaasen. There's no one funnier.

While we're at the beach, I finish the draft of what I think will be a book. I've reworked my Doctor of Ministry thesis, attempting to make a totally unreadable manuscript readable. I think academic study and experience in Congo are important, and I want people to pay attention. The church should be paying attention! Development organizations should be paying attention! Later, I send the manuscript to a couple of readers—a seminary professor and a writer in international development policy. I think they will be interested.

No interest.

Not even a "This sucks."

I get such great ideas while trying to do nothing on the beach. At least, they're great ideas on the beach, not so much off the beach.

Here's another great idea. I'd just finished 1,000 kilometers riding in the mountains of eastern Congo and got no notice. We had alerted everybody we knew who might be interested in the story, but there were no takers. We had gotten no traction, no publicity. I decided to take the show on the road. I would ride 1,000 miles around Indiana to match the 1,000 kilometers I had ridden around North Katanga. Maybe this would get some attention.

Heather Cress volunteers to organize the ride. She is married to a pastor of a congregation in Worthington, Indiana, and knows the area. She begins calling churches all over Indiana to let them know when I'll be in their area and find those who would let me couch surf.

Starting in New Harmony in the state's southwest corner, I head for Evansville. The roads down there are beautiful. In Evansville, I meet Steve Walker, who rides with me for a couple days. In the Indianapolis area, two other pastors ride with me on two different days, but the rest of the trip is solo.

In the beginning, the hospitality is generous, but by the second week, it gets thin. When I hit 1,000 miles on the odometer, I am in the middle of nowhere, somewhere in the northern half of the state, with open fields, impossible headwinds. I have missed the day's lunch date by hours, and I am done. I call Teri to come get me. She picks me up at the McDonalds on the interstate. Two weeks. 1,000 miles. Done.

The ride had produced one story in our conference newspaper but no buzz.

On this return, I've learned a hard truth: I cannot yet articulate what I've been learning. The gap between what the church thinks it is doing in mission and what I am seeing is too big, and I don't yet have the words to describe what I am seeing. I can see it, but I can't find words for it.

New York
Tanenbaum Center, October 2010

In October, I receive a phone call from Bishop Ntambo. He is to be honored by the Tanenbaum Center for Interreligious Understanding for his work as "Peacemaker in Action." (If the Nobel Peace Prize is the "Oscar" for philanthropic work, the Tanenbaum is the Tony.) The Bishop wants to know if I can come. Without hesitation, I book a flight to New York, along with a downtown hotel room, write the $250 donor check to the Tanenbaum Center, and show up in my best suit, with a clerical collar. I am totally out of my element—Upper East Side, 42nd floor, overlooking Central Park—but I find everyone to be incredibly nice people.

It is a fantastic night. We recount the heroic actions that the bishop and all the pastors and lay leaders at his command took to do the hard work of building peace during a horrific war. He and they are honored for courageously staying in place when the rest of the community leaders were running.

The Tanenbaum Center makes special recognition of the fact that the peace that Bishop Ntambo built was accomplished in an intentional interfaith effort. Even though he is a United Methodist bishop, Ntambo led a coalition of Catholics, Pentecostals, United Methodists, Muslims, Animists, and government and military leaders to the peace table.

Even the warlords came—the warlords who'd taught their young militia that they had the spiritual gift of immortality, that bullets would pass right through them harmlessly. These warlords came with their necklaces of human genitalia. This grim jewelry reflects that the terror of this war, a war in which women were publicly raped, and men were chopped up with machetes, cannot be understated. The Tanenbaum Center was honoring Bishop Ntambo for the incredible courage necessary to stand against this war.

The staff of the Tanenbaum Center is surprisingly ecumenical. There are Jewish leaders and an Episcopal bishop, a board member of the center, among others. Several members of Ntambo's family have been flown in for the celebration. A handful of personal friends, like me, are United Methodist. But there is something, someone, missing. There are no United Methodist bishops, no General Secretaries, no official representatives of the General Board of Global Ministries. I call them out specifically because their office is on Riverside Drive. They could have walked here. Moreover, there are no United Methodist journalists. The staff of the Tanenbaum Center is a bit confused, and the bishop is visibly hurt as he asks me why these people weren't there.

Maybe there was poor notification. I don't know. I had nothing to do with setting up the reception or ensuring that the right people got there. I am just a lowly pastor riding a bicycle in the field. The bishop does mention my recent tour by bicycle into the remote, war-torn districts in his acceptance speech, but it seems that he and I share the same publicist. I heard later that a presentation was made at the Council of Bishops meeting in Lake Junaluska. And there were articles written on the missions pages of denominational news outlets. The United Methodist Church's American leadership does not see what I saw. This award isn't a nice story about the denomination's missions in Africa. This is a remarkable story of the Church at its finest, at its bravest, and it should have been front-page news in United Methodist publications.

The US leaders of the denomination cannot see the Church at its very best because they are focused on lamenting its decline. Frustration at their inability to see burns me up inside. They spend all their time quarreling over how to reverse this decline at home. They do not see the United Methodist bishops, pastors, and lay leaders of the Church in the Congo and other parts of Africa as part of their church. Instead, they are the objects of American charity and pity, not colleagues and peers.

Maybe this is why I can't get excited about the big "wipe out malaria" campaigns. At this same time in 2010, the top leadership of The United Methodist Church and the lead pastors of the mega-churches are raising millions of dollars to eradicate disease among the poor of Africa. Yet they are completely failing to see the brave colleagues in the field already doing this work and suffering for lack of support. We are missing all of it.

My frustration drives me to keep speaking up, though, to keep drawing attention to the work my Congolese colleagues are already doing. So, I plan to go back.

London to Kitwe

January 2011

THIS SECOND FRIENDLY PLANET bicycle tour begins with flights from Indy to Chicago, then Chicago to London. I spend the day in London, riding the Tube into the city to make my pilgrimage once again to David Livingstone's tomb at Westminster Abbey. I'm careful to make it back in time for the evening flight to Lusaka, Zambia. I've done this many times, though, so I'm not too worried.

In Lusaka, my daughter Taylor picks me up at the airport. I spend a couple days with Taylor and her husband Stuart, who works in the American embassy there. From Lusaka to Lubumbashi, I'm on my own, traveling light with little more than a backpack and a new Canon T2 SLR camera. (I want to try to get some high-quality photos this time.)

Monday morning Stuart and Taylor drive Lusaka District Superintendent John Malomba and me to the Lusaka bus station to catch the early bus to the Copperbelt. We missed the first 6:30 bus—it had departed on time. We did catch the 2nd 6:30 bus; it was running 15 minutes behind. My oversized bicycle case, a hard-shell suitcase, and a plastic storage box are quickly loaded in the undercarriage, and off we go. John's English is about equivalent to my French. Both of us are more interested in sleeping, so there is not much conversation. I read and doze. After riding about six hours (with a couple rest stops), we are let out on the side of the road not far from the Kafakumba Training Center. In a few minutes, a truck arrives to pick us up. Bill, the driver, is a retired Delphi automotive engineer from Kokomo, Indiana. Small world.

London to Kitwe

The drive from Lusaka to Lubumbashi can be made in a day, but Monday is the worst day of the week to cross the border, and we don't want to be on the road after darkness falls. It gets dark early here. So we layover at Kafakumba.

Kafakumba is the life's work of John Enright, a United Methodist missionary serving in the region since the early 1970s. During the war in Congo, John and his wife Kendra relocated across the border to Zambia. There they established the Kafakumba Training Center, named after the pastor's school John's father had begun in the Congo many years ago.

Standing next to his truck, John and I engage in one of his famous political/theological *chautauquas*. Mostly John talks, and I occasionally try to say something not too stupid. Today's lesson is that international aid is poison. John's goal is for the mission station to be self-sufficient and not reliant upon donors in the United States.

At Kafakumba, Pastor John Malomba hands me off to Pastor Robert Malimba, the Bishop's Assistant in Zambia. I join his family for a delicious home-cooked meal full of local flavors. Robert's wife is also named Teresa, and they have four delightful children. Tuesday morning, Robert and I take a taxi for the two-hour drive to the border at Kasumbalesa.

On the way, we drive through Kitwe, and I am reminded of being here after the United Methodist missionaries were evacuated from the Democratic Republic of the Congo in 1998. We had been resettled for a couple weeks while lives and jobs were sorted out. I hadn't wanted to leave Likasi, our home in the DRC. I had been there on the General Board of Global Ministries' payroll, but I was at odds with their leadership. I was tired of the reputation that United Methodist missionaries had earned for fleeing every time there was a threat of war. I made my case with the district leaders that I should stay. But they feared that the bishop would hold them responsible for my safety—a responsibility that I'm still learning to understand—and voted that I should leave with the other missionaries. My American boss came from New York to meet with all the evacuated missionaries. Speaking with him one-on-one, I said, "If they had decided that they wanted me to stay, I would have stayed. You would have fired me. And we both would have been right." No one can serve two masters.

Some evacuated missionaries already had places to go and things to do, and some needed new job assignments. Eventually, I was the only one left. There was an open job in Kitwe as a chaplain at the Mindolo Ecumenical Foundation, a community development and peace and governance education institution established by the World Council of Churches back in the '60s. I was shoehorned into that position.

For the next several months, I was in charge of weekday morning chapel services for over two hundred people. It was there that I gave up on learning French and Swahili, as no one there spoke either. On weekends, I had no responsibilities. Unlike in the Congo, where everyone wanted me to come and speak at their church on Sundays, I was ignored. When Holy Week came, I found myself not invited to any church, and I realized that that was the first Easter in my entire life that I would spend outside the church looking in. I was a bit sad for not feeling wanted but mostly felt relieved not to have any responsibility. I wound up spending the weekend in solitary reflection.

There were places in and around town that I had never seen simply because I had had no reason to go there. So, on Saturday afternoon, I got on my bicycle, started riding with no particular place to go, and allowed the roads to lead me. There was the Polo Club, a leftover from colonial days. Then there was the Nkana East miners' cemetery. It was clear that it had once been tree-lined and groomed with a small maintenance building built to resemble a chapel. In 1999, it had only half a roof. The grass was raggedly cut, and the road and paths showed little maintenance. I guessed that the families of those buried there were long gone. Checking the names on the stones confirmed my suspicion that this was a "white" cemetery. Makes sense. The mining industry brought white settlers to Kitwe— then called Nkana—in the early twentieth century.

By chance, I went to the section of graves of people who died in 1952, the year of my birth. It was a strange sensation of time. The marked graves I saw mostly belonged to people who died in their 40s, but most of the graves are unmarked now, just four holes and a shadow where the brass plaque had been. I was struck by how easily we can be forgotten once we leave a place. It was a difficult thought to entertain while I was being forced to leave the DRC.

Now in 2011, I'm just passing through Kitwe. No bike rides around town, no conversations with missionaries. I make my way to Kasumbelesa, the first town over the border into DRC, by bus and taxi, with a lot of help from friends. When Pastor Robert and I get to the border, District Superintendent Joseph Mulongo is there on the Zambian side. He had been traveling for three days to meet me at the border and take over the task of keeping me out of trouble. My bicycle case is a curiosity at customs, but no one can find a reason to deny it or even charge for it. When they discover that I am a United Methodist pastor, most Congolese officials treat me with respect and welcome me to the country.

Mulongo had rented a van to get us to Lubumbashi. The road from Kasumbalesa to Lubumbashi is all-new, Chinese built. No problems.

In Lubumbashi, I stay at the Methodist Guest House, run by Mama Odia. I've been staying in this house since 1991. This house is a constant amidst the changes in Congo. We'll be here until we have all the official papers and provisions we need to go upcountry. From here, we'll be headed to the mining town of Tenke.

Tenke

January 2011

WE'RE PULLING THE TEAM together for a second tour. As in 2010, this tour begins in Tenke. The bus ride from Lubumbashi to Tenke has become routine. As in 2010, Prospere, Shabana, and Éléphant will be joining us. New to the ride are Pastor Kora and Daniel Mumba.

Kora has been down at Africa University in Zimbabwe working on a Master's in Theology. We've invited Kora along because he was one of the pastors who'd worked with Bishop Ntambo to bring the warlords to the peace summit in 2004. His experience during the war will be invaluable to us on this trip as we make our way all the way to Kabalo, deep in the war zone. He's one of the pastors who stayed in place with their communities when everyone else was running, and I'm looking forward to hearing his stories.

I'm still in a non-directive mode. I couldn't direct if I wanted to. I can't tell people what to do, and I certainly can't explain why I would want something done the way I wanted it done. This feels uncomfortable at times, and I know it is strange for my Congolese colleagues, too. But this is the discipline of the process, no matter how uncomfortable we all are.

Daniel Mumba is now the district superintendent of the Tenke District and, therefore, my host in Tenke. Mumba is also a close friend of Mulongo from their time as classmates at Mulungwishi Seminary. Professionally, Mulongo acts as a mentor for Mumba in The United Methodist Church, and personally, their families are close. Mumba and I have an interesting exchange of gifts: I sleep under his roof and eat the food his wife prepares for me. He gets the prestige of hosting me. Even though what I am doing is not yet understood by anyone, everyone assumes that those connected to this project will benefit. That's how things work in a patronage society. Because I'm white, because I'm an American, because I'm a missionary, I have prestige; therefore, I must also have resources. If I play my role as expected, the people closest to me will get some of those resources and some of my prestige. It's a role that makes me uncomfortable. Sometimes I resist it. Sometimes I try to use it to change the system.

Mumba believes that his district is the smallest and least important of all the districts of North Katanga. He doesn't yet see what I see: the Tenke District is strategically located for development and has access to resources that others do not have. It is the home of the Tenke-Fungarume Mine: an Anglo-American mining company. This mine is qualitatively different from other mines in the region because TFM uses industry-standard practices. Entering the mine property is like leaving a war-ravaged nation for a first-class neighborhood. While I'm not a fan of the mines in general, this mine is exceptional. It takes its contract with the government to be a good community partner seriously, including building schools and residential housing. In 2009, TFM had built a water project on the property of the United Methodist Church: three huge water tanks that trucks filled daily. Coming back after just two years, I found the tanks gone and replaced by a spring-fed bank of public taps, providing plenty of water for the whole community.

Part of Friendly Planet Missiology's goal is to help local leaders build these kinds of partnerships with the other entities in their communities. But first, they have to see the possibilities and to do that, they have to let go of the old models.

Bishop Ntambo sent us a message that our team should wait in Tenke to host a team coming from the US. We were to hold up our tour until these visitors arrived, and that's all we knew.

We put together after the fact that these visitors planned on going to Kamina, but there was no way to get them there. The pilot Gaston was in the States, so the Bishop figured that he could send them to Tenke, and I could take care of them. No biggie, glad to help, as long as we didn't end up waiting a week for someone who never showed.

But they did show. Two men from Kansas City—a pastor and a layperson from the Church of the Resurrection, the largest United Methodist church in the US. Good guys. Fun to be with. Although, they flew all the way to the Congo and were barely off the plane before holding their breath until they got back to "civilization." One of them had such serious food concerns that he carried his own tuna fish packets. They were still good people, and if I had my druthers, I'd take them over most who come as volunteers.

The pastor had heard Bishop Ntambo talk in Ft. Worth and was convinced of the need for Bibles in North Katanga. He was recruited as a mission pastor at the Church of the Resurrection, and when he went there, he brought along his passion for this project. He and a lay traveling companion brought along 300 Kiluba Bibles, along with a half dozen audio Bible players.

Coincidentally— or providentially—North Katanga's two conference evangelists were also in Tenke for an evangelism seminar. Evangelists in the Congo are different from evangelists in the US. When I think of evangelists in the US, I think of anti-intellectual, emotion-filled preachers. In North Katanga, it is the opposite: the two conference evangelists are the leading Biblical scholars in the conference.

One of the conference evangelists, Guy Nyembo Kinkundulu, had been the assistant director of the Likasi School of Theology when I was the director (dean) back in the '90s. He still lives in Likasi, even though the seminary is closed. Now Nyembo teaches Hebrew and Greek at the Lutheran Seminary in Lubumbashi. There aren't many Lutheran churches in the Congo, but they do have a seminary. Go figure. Mbayo Mujinga, the other conference evangelist, worked on the 25-year-long joint project of United Methodists and Pentecostals to translate the Bible into Kiluba. The Bibles in those boxes are the result of his work.

The plan was to distribute the Bibles to those who completed the evangelism seminar, but it didn't go down that way. It all went so very wrong. The distribution happened during worship on Sunday. Before it could be stopped, every one of the 300 Bibles had been passed out to whoever was there. It was chaos. A happy chaos, but chaos, nonetheless. When I posted photos of the happy worshippers with their new Bibles, a Congolese colleague studying in the U. S. commented, "I know that that mama can't read." We gave out a lot of Bibles to people who can't read.

There's an even bigger problem than giving Bibles to people who can't read, though. Out in the bush, in the remote districts that don't have direct bus service from Lubumbashi, we have over 900 churches that don't have Bibles. I'm not talking about churches that don't have pew Bibles: these are churches in communities where there is not a single Bible. Pastors gather with pastors from other villages and other denominations to access materials for sermon preparation. In worship, choirs teach the people biblical stories through song.

With 900 churches without a Bible, we just gave out 300 Bibles in one day in one church. Not smart, but lesson learned. This was our bad. The Church of the Resurrection did a good thing in preparing their generous gift of 300 Bibles. As the United Methodist leadership on the ground in Tenke, we failed to prep the project for effectiveness. Even though it was sprung on us, and we had no idea what was going on until they arrived with the Bibles, we could have done better.

This is an important reminder to all those traveling to foreign places seeking to do good: your efforts could be made effective if people like us prep the community before you come. It's our job to get both you and the community ready. In this case, we weren't prepared for the delivery of 300 Bibles.

I've spent some time with North Katanga's conference evangelists, getting to know them and their program better. I'm impressed with them as leaders and teachers and convinced that their program has merit. Let me go so far as saying that their program has the potential for major transformation in North Katanga, both in the United Methodist churches and more widely in the communities. I argue that the best way to improve the health and welfare of villages is to invest in their evangelistic program. Want a village to have safe drinking water? Support this team of evangelists. And I don't say this because the conference evangelists and Friendly Planet are on the same denominational team. No, trust me: the work they do will have longer-lasting effects than any direct public health project, and it will be faster.

The conference evangelists have an unfunded mandate. Their job is to take their evangelism seminar to all the districts, but they don't have the money for the program or even their own salaries. They have asked if they can use our boat. Their program would be the best use of our boat, but I don't know how we would fund it. We're talking at least a $50,000 project.

Here's my trickster way of getting you to fund it. I know from experience that churches won't give money for an evangelism project, even evangelical type churches. People will, however, give money for Bibles. So, here's the deal. We can buy these Kiluba Bibles in Lubumbashi for $12 each. Transportation costs upcountry will run the cost up to $20 or $25. Doubling that cost to $50 per Bible would allow us to deliver the Bible in a training program that would transform the whole North Katanga Conference.

Less than that, and we'd be wasting your money. Sure, $25 would pay to get Bibles to the DRC, and the people who receive the Bibles will be overjoyed. Good Christians in the US will be proud of spreading the Word. But for $50 a Bible, we could help change the world. In a matter of a couple years, communities would be strong enough to address all their social and health issues.

If you're not particularly evangelical or even religious, you might be wondering how evangelism impacts community development. In the US, the separation of church and state is not only constitutionally mandated; it is lived out in everyday life, even among conservative Christians. There are things that the church does and things that the church does not do. Maybe the church will have a food pantry, but you don't see the church training people in farming. 4H and FFA and the Purdue Extension Office do that.

In the DRC, the church is involved in all aspects of community life. And not just involved: the church is the trusted leader in community development. This evangelism program can increase that leadership role into a more effective church leadership network. The evangelism program is more about organizing the work than about mass rallies. It creates a platform for all community transformation. In the preaching of the evangelists, we hear the call to change the way we are doing things.

Church Visits around Tenke

MUMBA HAS A WEEK of church visits planned for us in his district before we can take off for Mulongo. His vision for these visits amounts to a traveling district conference, including the celebration of holy communion and baptisms. I'm not comfortable with being the star of the parade. OK, that's a lie. Who am I trying to kid? I love being the star of the parade. I love a good parade, and I love being the grand marshal. However, I know in my heart and head that any community development plan built around me and my presence will fail. If I'm the solution to the community's problems, the solution goes with me when I leave.

It's not that I couldn't solve their problems. I'm actually pretty smart, and I see solutions everywhere. A side of me would love to settle in a particular village and lead them to health and prosperity. Even as I say this, I hope you can hear how dysfunctional that sounds. It's the God complex. If you've never seen the movie *At Play in the Fields of the Lord*, you must. It's the best missionary training video I know.

Mumba has set up a bicycle tour through his district featuring me as the missionary coming to serve the people communion and baptize their children. This traveling district conference is a real challenge to my own rules. By refusing to interfere in how my missiology plays out, I'm about to violate my own missiology in the process. There is a great temptation to say to Mumba, "I shouldn't be the one doing all these baptisms; you should be doing them." But this is his plan, and this is how he wants to use me. He's cashing in my celebrity for the mission. I might question his personal motives—this will undoubtedly elevate his status in his district and in the conference—but we all have mixed motives, and this is his plan for lifting the district's morale.

Our parade takes off from Tenke, riding toward Dikanda. I find my place behind the district lay leader on his beat-up old bicycle. There is a constant metal on metal clinking coming from his bike. It's almost musical. I think, "Noise on a bicycle means inefficiency. A fast bike is a quiet bike. He's riding an old rattletrap." But that's not what's happening: it's not his bicycle that's making the noise. The clinking is the sound of the district communion set in the bag on the back of his bike.

This revelation changes my whole attitude. Our team is carrying communion to these villages in the trays of a hand-me-down, pot metal communion set, donated by some church in Indiana—a set no longer needed and sent to Africa. Some old saint died and left a church a thousand dollars for a new communion set, so they put this one away in a closet. It was in that closet when Bishop Ntambo visited, and they packed it up and gave it to him, along with twenty old, worn-out choir robes. Such is church life in the Congo: secondhand communion sets and secondhand robes.

The role of the district superintendent in the Congo is old-school Methodist, and the traveling elder is still the norm. The sacraments are brought to the villages, and communion and baptism are district-level practices of the Church, rather than something a local congregation would do on their own. This sounds a bit strange to Americans, even Methodist Americans. Here, it's just how it's done.

As we ride, I realize that my role in this drama is not so much the foreign missionary but the traveling elder. While the villagers don't see it this way—they see a white missionary—Mumba's understanding counts here. Bringing the sacraments to local congregations defines the elder's job. To Mumba and Kora, we are a team of traveling elders out doing our job. And I can see how much they enjoy this.

Dikanda is on a river, but I don't know which river. Eventually, all the rivers run into the Lualaba, which becomes the Congo River. Well, all except those that run south to Zambia. But as we are in the area where the watershed shifts, it's possible this river runs south. Beats me. I have no idea where we are, anyway. The people who live here say that there are still hippos in the marshy grass between the village and the river. So I know that much—it's a river with hippos. We notice that a bridge has recently been repaired. They tell us that these repairs happened because a crocodile killed a child who was wading across the river. As is the case in the US, critical infrastructure maintenance gets delayed too long; only tragedy makes things happen.

We are housed in the school, which is on break, and I'm given the headmaster's office. This school is funded by the mine and is well built—brick walls, concrete floors, and tin roofs. The textbooks on the shelves of the headmaster's office include health books. The books are high quality, French language, Belgian published, modern health books made especially for the Congo. No second-hand books in English, cast off from American schools and packed into shipping containers for the poor children of Africa. These are up-to-date French language textbooks specific to Africa. This is what we need. Congolese problems are not going to be solved with hand-me-downs. It will take a first-class, detailed, and strategic curriculum. I'm looking at just that.

I'm reading a middle school health textbook on how cholera is spread.

This bicycle tour is not a stand-alone program, though. What we are celebrating is not simply the coming of a missionary. The Tenke District has been engaged in a year-long evangelism emphasis. These sacraments we will celebrate are the celebration of a year's work.

In Dikanda, we did the first of the baptisms—26 of them. We even filled out and signed baptismal certificates. The district superintendents and other traveling elders carry a tear-out coupon book for all pastoral contacts, including communion and baptism. I think this is way cool. Elders visit a church member in a remote village, fill out a coupon, and give it to them. The villager puts it among their valuable papers, maybe even tapes it on the wall of their living room.

These coupons become a record of relationships. One chief tells us proudly that he was baptized by Bishop Booth. Newell Booth was an American who came to the Belgian Congo as a missionary in the 1930s and ultimately became the Methodist bishop here. Under his leadership, Methodist churches proliferated, and church leaders became integral to civic leadership. We have to recognize his role in creating the congregations we're visiting. The people we baptized on this trip will be proud of their connection to us. They'll say, "I was baptized by Pastor Bob." I'm not really comfortable with that. But it's part of the role of traveling elder that Mumba has chosen for me on this trip.

By the time we get to the third village, we have run out of coupons, and I'm sorry about that.

Rain holds us up for a day. When the rain has quit, we get back on the road. Kora teaches me the African saying, "It's easy to ride in the rain; it's the day after the rain that is hard." And hard it is. The mud is so thick that we are constantly stopping to dig it out of our fenders. I think it would be better to sling the mud up my back, and I question the wisdom of having fenders on the bicycle. Fenders are an accessory that I have because everyone thinks that I should, but I'm not convinced. They seem like nothing but trouble.

Outside Dikanda, we're in farmland—land belonging to a commercial farm with large cornfields and a blue Ford tractor, a big one. We stop and talk with the driver and his friends working in the field. I ask for permission and take their pictures.

At the end of the road south, one valley over from Zambia, we come to an old farm plantation. It is still a running commercial farm owned by the governor and/or his friends. The grand colonial plantation manor is in decay but still makes for good photos. I'm shown a room in a modest guest house, which is not fancy, but it is clean and dry. The room comes with a mosquito bed net, new, never been used, still in the plastic bag, marked "from the people of the United States of America." I chuckled. I wonder how many bed nets have never gotten to their intended recipients but are hoarded by the upper class for their guest houses.

The Kipendano (The United Methodist Women) cook for us in a tiny hole-in-the-wall kitchen in the guest house. I capture them in some of my favorite photos. They're a hospitable bunch.

The village church is under construction. Well, not really. It's more of a dream of construction. Under the pastor's leadership, the community has collected rocks for the foundation and shaped and fired bricks. Currently, the rocks sit in one pile, and the bricks lay still in the kiln used to fire them. So, instead of in the church, we meet in the school classroom. Packed with people, it is hot and steamy. I can barely see for the humidity in the room. The water vapor collects on my glasses. We perform more baptisms. This village needs to build a church.

Next village. More baptisms. Another Kipendano meal. I watch the village children playing. The brooms here don't have broomsticks; they're made of a handful of straw tied about a third of the way down. You can bunch the broom on the ground, and the straw spreads out so that the broom stands on its own. The children are bouncing the broom on the ground and jumping over it. I wonder if this is the origin of "jumping the broom." Is that broom meant to be more like this broom?

A great commotion comes from the other side of the village. A snake! Children are running and screaming. The snake is taken seriously. No one is interested in playing with it, and all the children run away. Two of the men kill the snake with extreme prejudice. It's a green mamba—deadly.

Church Visits around Tenke

In the end, I have to apologize for misjudging Mumba's missiological insight. Though it is not at all what I would have planned, it turns out to be perfect. The Democratic Republic of the Congo is a super religious country, and it is overwhelmingly Christian. Evangelism is not for conversion from a different religion or from no religion; it is a calling of people out of their poverty into the salvation of God in Jesus Christ. Here's the trick and the question that drives this book: Is their trust in Jesus for deliverance from this poverty working for them?

Carrying the Robe and Collar

THE LAST THING YOU'D think of carrying on a bicycle would be a preaching robe, but it's important enough for me to find a place for one. As a sign of the office, robes are essential. Pastors in the bush barely have a decent shirt, so having something to wear in the pulpit on Sunday that elevates the pastor's status in the community is vital.

One of the problems we face in leadership development in the Congolese Methodist hierarchy is the issue of status. Living wage jobs are extremely rare, and most folks live in what they themselves know to be undignified conditions. So the drive to seek honored status and financial resources is especially strong. In the Congo, as is true around the world, people pursue jobs for the status they provide as well as for the salary or potential for exploitation. Many become pastors with hopes of acquiring a congregation's resources and becoming a "Big Man" in the village. This dynamic is well-known to the church hierarchy and the laypeople. I've had congregants say to me that their pastor is in ministry for the wrong reasons. Not enough people seem to understand their appointment is a task to be done as a service to the community. In an economy built on patronage, this is to be expected, but it still frustrates me.

When I was directing the seminary in Likasi in 1998, I taught a class on leadership for those who were about to graduate and receive their first appointments. Their student stipends were not adequate to feed their families, and after graduation, they would go to communities where they would be paid even less than they were receiving as students. They would need to stock up on everything they were going to need for a life-long ministry of and in poverty. So, we tried to equip the graduates with some basics—a travel trunk, a rain barrel, a bicycle, a suit for the men, and a dress for the women. Fabric was purchased locally, and the suits and dresses were made by the women of our Foyer, a women's school for the wives of the student pastors who were mostly men. They each already had a Bible.

So, one day in the leadership class, a student asked, "We were taught that there is a different color for each season of the liturgical year. Could we not be given different colored robes for every season?"

I just lost it.

Upon reflection, maybe the student got the word wrong and meant stoles, or maybe I got the translation wrong and heard robes; in any case, I lost it and exploded on the class, "You know that our ministry is not about robes. It is about service."

I launched into a lecture on servant ministry and attacked those who only saw the ministry as a status to be exploited. The class was stunned. No one had ever yelled at them that way. The next day I apologized.

Since then, I've been walking down a road of reflection with that clergy robe. I've been trying to think through the complexity of the role of the pastor in the community and how we can best equip and support these underpaid servants of God.

I'm not immune to the attraction of status as a pastor. I know the motivations behind a calling to the ministry are messy.

The value of elevated status for pastors was evident to me on one visit to a new church start in Lubudi. The sanctuary was not finished, and the congregation was meeting in a house with a large living room. They were packed in, but as the pastor and I made our way down the center of the crowd, the congregation stood for us. This is still done in many African-American congregations, and you may remember the courthouse scene in *To Kill a Mockingbird*, "Stand up, Scout. Your father's passing." As for Scout standing for her father, Atticus Finch, standing up is a demonstration of respect when the pastor passes through the congregation. Mostly, this is not a bad thing, but it requires that the pastor feel worthy of the respect. In 2005, I was doing some interviews with 20 pastors in the Kamina District who were serving poor villages. Their lack of decent clothing shamed them. They were not able to stand before their congregations in rags. Their lack of even a good shirt brought shame on the church.

So, I carry a robe to show respect to the pastors we visit and to not force any of them to give up their robe for the visiting missionary. My travel robe is not an expensive one. It's the single-use one that was provided for my Doctor of Ministry graduation ceremony. If I ever wash it or dry clean it, it will dissolve. This robe joins a blue dress shirt with a clerical collar, and a stole in a flat compression bag tucked into one of my bicycle's rear panniers.

Pastors, Chiefs, and Warlords

The Second Tour

January–March 2011
Tenke to Mulongo

ONCE WE FINISH MUMBA's parade route around Tenke, we set off for Mulongo. The riding this year seems much easier than it was in 2010. The road has been worked on a bit. There's not as much rain as last year. But mostly, I'm in better shape, and we know the road now. We're beginning to know what we're doing.

We head for Mulongo.

It will take seven days.

Fungarume

As we ride through Fungarume, we run into an officer of the Agence Nationale de Renseignements (ANR) who takes it upon himself to challenge my existence. The ANR is Congo's national intelligence agency, responsible for internal security, including immigration. They issue documents for internal travel, and wherever I go, I must check in with them. I know that traveling along the Red Road means there may be checkpoints where I'll need to show my documents.

I've been hassled in the past by police or soldiers in the street, but it's usually something that I've been able to handle myself. Once, in Likasi, a soldier with an AK47 stopped me and asked me to give him my backpack; he admired it and wanted it. I laughed and acted as if he were just joking, and I walked on. He had to remain at his post as I put a healthy distance between us. Since this was my normal route to work, I saw him the next day and greeted him with a big smile.

Another time in Kamina, I was in the commercial district by myself at night when a police officer, clearly drunk, insisted I show him my passport. Because of his drunken state and because I knew that this was neither the time nor place for such a challenge, I refused. My plan was to let myself be arrested and sort it out at the police station. As I expected, the drunk policeman wasn't interested in pursuing the case at the station.

Usually, however, I'm not on my own, and I hang back and allow my friends to handle the situation. This challenge is highly irregular and feels like a shakedown, so I watch from a safe distance, standing over my bicycle, as Kora takes the lead. As he talks the ANR agent out of his need to see my papers, my imagination hears him saying, "These aren't the droids you're looking for."

And we're on our way again.

We spend the first night at Mulungwishi. Mid-morning of day two, we turn north at Lwambo and head for Mulongo. We set up our tents in a little village with no name. We stopped here on last year's ride, and the feeling of familiarity is good.

The bike ride is easy and fast. We'll be in Mulongo in good time.

Kyubo

DURING THE WAR, KYUBO was overrun by multiple armies and militias. Homes, schools, and churches were burned to the ground. Hundreds in the village were killed, and those not killed fled into the forest, where they struggled to find food and shelter. The UN estimated the destruction of villages along the Red Road like Kyubo to be at the 80% level.

This is the dilemma: this community had been totally beaten down and struggling to rebuild social structures, barely able to make it to the next day. Outsiders look at this community and see ignorant primitives, but they're wrong. The community is intelligent and innovative. In fact, I'm impressed with the project proposals that are presented to me. They can do this work, but they are exhausted. I feel the exhaustion just thinking about the work that needs to be done. They need help now.

This all reminds me once more of the contrast in the messages I bring to different audiences. At home in the States, I say to people, "We've got to get some real help to these people, and we've got to get it to them now. They're dying." In Congo, I say, "Everything we need, God has already provided. We have sufficient resources right here to rebuild our communities."

When the FPM team was here one year ago, civic structures had started to recover—we were met by a parade of Boy Scouts and church choirs—but physical structures were still in ruins. People were living in simple grass huts or the ruined remains of where their homes used to be. The church at Kyubo was a mere footprint in the tall grass with three wooden crosses in front.

In 2011, we find further progress. The walls of the new church are up. The construction committee meets with us, asking for assistance to get the needed cement and roofing to complete the building. We don't promise, but we don't say "no," which is the same as promising.

The resort in Kyubo is also making progress and is almost ready to open. The manager of the construction phase is gone, and a new manager has arrived for the start-up phase. This new manager is Congolese and is much more welcoming than the South African construction manager we met last year. Besides being Congolese, the new construction manager is also United Methodist. There's no doubt in my mind where the money for the construction of the new church is coming from.

The manager welcomes us and several members of the church for a tour of the resort. This is probably the only time, unless they work here, that the church members are going to see such wealth. There is a delightful playfulness among the group as we walk around the decks connecting the grass-roofed lodges and overlooking the river and the falls. Photo opportunities abound. The rooms are not finished, so we don't get to sleep in luxury, but we are put up in the staff tent, bunk room style. It is the best bed I'll sleep in for some time.

Kasengeshi

AT KASENGESHI, WE ARE invited to an audience with the Grand Chief. This slows us down a full half-day but is worth the time lost. This chief lives well above the poverty level of his community. We wait inside the wall of his compound under the shelter of a paillotte, a large, circular grass-roofed outdoor space for lounging and meeting. High-ranking people build them so they can meet with visitors and offer shade without bringing strangers into private family spaces. This house also has both electricity and internet connections. When the chief comes out, there are Cokes and Fantas served, and we have the nice talk mandated by protocol. Then he gets serious about why he wanted to meet with me.

On the internet, the Chief has seen a portable mining machine that works in small rivers. He wants one to extract the gold that is in the stream coming down the local mountains. Fed up with the foreign mining companies coming in and stealing all the gold, he wants the mines' wealth to stay in the local community for development. He wants me to set up an NGO that would be a community-based mining company. He gives me two bags of minerals, one of coltan and one of tin, but no gold.

I'm intrigued. But I can also imagine the nightmare of trying to compete with the big boys for the gold in these hills. There are armies from Rwanda and Uganda invading for this gold (and for the coltan). Scary strongmen politicians are running the world far above my pay grade. This goes all the way to the UN.

What goes on in mining is way over my head, and I see entering into that game as a trap. Tempting, but a sucker's bet. One time, Joseph Mulongo and I were crossing the Congo River by pirogue. At the same time, cargo from a truck was being offloaded onto the ferry on one side. It was a ten-ton truckload of bags of coltan, each about half the size of a bag of cement.

The two dozen men doing the loading were young, lean, strong, Black, and shirtless, their upper bodies pouring sweat.

When the ferry was loaded, they got into the water and swam the ferry across the river because the motor no longer worked. On the other bank, the same men loaded the bags onto another waiting truck. I asked Mulongo, "Where does the coltan go from here?" He shrugged his shoulders and said, "Moise knows." (Moise's the governor.)

Millions have already been killed over the gold and coltan. Setting up a mining NGO would be as stupid as my trying to set up a drug-running business in Columbia. Nevertheless, the chief has a point: if only someone could find a way to run a small mining company for the good of the community...

An idea strikes. Back in Terre Haute, Indiana, in the days of my youth, there was a business called the Gibson Coal Company. My family was working class, but we knew the Gibsons well. Mom was a close friend from grade school of the daughter, and my aunt had a career as LaVern Gibson's secretary. The Gibson Coal Company didn't own coal mines; they owned trucks. They were a *trucking* company. The idea is taking shape. We can be the Friendly Planet Missiology and Mining Company, but we won't own mines. We'll run a trucking company.

Mitwaba

Rain pours on us as we ride up to Mitwaba, the wild west of mining towns in the high country. The team is soaked when we stop at the home of the United Methodist pastor for a meal and a chance to wash up. I am offered a "shower"—a bucket of water in a small outroom with a drain in the floor. There I find a bar of soap on a brick and a towel hanging on the door. When I return, Éléphant is drying his socks over a charcoal fire. I get my socks and shoes out to dry.

Prospere's motorcycle is in pieces as he tries to rebuild the wheel. I'm not convinced that it is going to continue with us.

It's late, and I'm taken to the Catholic guest house, a converted office building, for the night. The bedroom is a large room with several beds separated from one another by bookshelves and wardrobes for privacy. With an outdoor toilet, this guesthouse is clean, safe, and comfortable.

The next day, we cross over the Mother of Mountains.

Crossing the Mother of Mountains has come to be the challenge that defines our rides. Today, I'm up to the challenge. It's raining. I put on my yellow rain jacket, but the rain is not unwelcome. It feels good. Cool.

The uphills are hard work. On the steep climbs, Éléphant still helps me, but I'm not desperate for his help, just thankful. My respect for him grows. He carries my heavy load without ever giving up a bit of personal dignity. This is what servant leadership looks like.

The downhills are scary. I still marvel at how reckless the others are. It's all I can do to hang on and try to control my speed and point the bike to avoid the sharp rocks. Twice the mountain beats me. I run out of brake and out of control. Scared shitless, I ride the bike into the upside of the mountain, choosing to run into the mountain rather than off the mountain. More embarrassed than hurt, I struggle to right the loaded bike and get back on. The road is much steeper than it looks, and the weight of the bike seems to be doubled by the gravity of the mountain. (Hey, I've had enough physics to know how dumb that statement is, but I don't have enough upper body strength to muscle the bike into control.)

Back up and rolling, the speed picks up again. The gravel of the road has been washed away, exposing the limestone bedrock. There are flat sections, slick and shining in the wet, slick and dangerous. Shortly, I'm once more out of brake and out of control. Then there are sections where the edges of these limestone slabs present themselves as knife edges. Running out of good choices, I run straight at the knife edges and blow out both tires. No options now; I ride the two flats down until I can find a place to fall.

Éléphant is quick to my rescue. He changes both tires. The tubes are shreds. One back tire needs replacing. We decide to use one of the two spare tires folded up in my panniers. With new treads, I walk most of the 3,000 feet to the bottom.

We camp at the foot of the mountain. It's two more days into Mulongo, but an easy ride. I recognize Kyolo and the fork in the road from our previous journey—it's the only decision we make in 300 kilometers.

We slip into Mulongo with little fanfare. It's home. I'm staying with Dr. Serge, the Congolese director of the British Brethren hospital in this village. I settle once again in the bedroom that now feels like my room.

From Bicycles to a Boat

Joseph writes:

Since the 2010 tour, we had been thinking about how to go to Pastor Jackie Mwayuma, who was appointed in Kabalo in the war zone in a very difficult time. Kabalo is one of the districts that was devastated by the war, where rape and murder were used as weapons by rebels, by militias, and even by government soldiers. Mama Mwayuma took the time to work with the women, not only in the church as the district superintendent but with everybody in the community, and she did much. We could not take the risk of riding our bicycles while the Mai Mai militia were operating actively in the Tanganyika area. The only way we could reach Mwayuma was by the river.

We decided, Bob raised the money, and we bought the *Indiana*. It became a mobile clinic, an ambulance, and a barge to deliver construction equipment. The *Indiana* was doing everything. When we went to Kabalo, Bob said that it was very important to go to encourage Mwayuma and to see the work she was doing and to try to do what we can do. We decided to make the adventure to Kabalo by boat. When we arrived in Mulongo, we parked our bicycles, we parked our motorcycles, and the team rearranged itself. Shabana and Prospére returned home to their families, Éléphant remained with us, and we took on some church leaders who needed transportation to Kabalo. It was like [Henry] Morton Stanley traveling to look for Dr. Livingstone. Dr. Bob was headed to Kabalo to look for Mama Mwayuma, the district superintendent who was lost in the war zone, who had not been seen for so many years.

When we arrived in Kabalo, we were not in need of someone to tell us the story of how Kabalo was destroyed. We saw the mark of violence on everything. We saw the mark of war even on people's faces. But Bob's arrival was received by Mama Mwayumba and all her team with great joy.

The Boat Arrives

THE BOAT IS HERE, and it's beautiful. About 25 feet long (I'm pretty bad at judging length). The name *UM Indiana*, the Friendly Planet Missiology logo, and the cross and flame of the North Katanga Diocese, Église Méthodiste-Unie, identify this boat's affiliations. The hull is Indianapolis Colts blue and white. There is even a horseshoe on the bow. The paint scheme is all a surprise to me. I had not asked for any special favors or offered any suggestions.

On the deck of the boat, a blue tarp over a frame of two by fours forms a canopy that shades six folding chairs. It looks like some tourist boat on the Zambezi ready to go out and look at hippos. The coolest feature is on the backs of the chairs: the Friendly Planet Missiology logo, stenciled by a design shop in Lubumbashi.

I am so proud! Everything was either made locally or sourced locally. We didn't ship a single thing from the States. The items that traveled the furthest are the bright orange life vests that Mulongo's brother-in-law brought over from Tanzania. The crew loves wearing them. It gives the boat and crew the look of professionalism.

Éléphant mans the tiller of the Yamaha outboard motor with a smile on his face. I've never seen a man look so content in what he is doing. He is oozing joy out of his whole self. He is one of a handful of friends whose happiness and success in their endeavors have become a goal in my life.

Taylor and I have had this conversation many times. What if our only mission is to support Joseph Mulongo's mission? After all, this is the bottom line of our missiology. Our primary goal is not to wipe out malaria, feed the children, or stop the war. It's not to build churches, schools, or clinics. It's to befriend and support a small group of visionary leaders to assist in making a dream a reality. But not our dream—*their* dream.

Our missiology is a corruption of the "starfish thrower," a mission model that I have come to believe is bankrupt. In case you've not heard it, the Starfish Thrower is the story of a person walking along a beach throwing stranded starfish back into the ocean. The beach is full of dying starfish, so the task is monumental, even undoable. More starfish are washing up on the beach even as the person throws starfish back. An observer says to the starfish thrower, "What's the use? You can't save them all."

"I can save this one," the starfish thrower responds as he throws another starfish back into the ocean.

This is probably the most popular of missionary stories, and it is compelling. For the individual who receives the help, it is, of course, life-giving. However, from a community development perspective, this model leads to more deaths in the long term, not fewer.

A pastor friend in Indiana who invites us for mission Sundays always introduces us with this story. I want to scream, "This is not what we are about! Just the opposite!" But I know that the people would not understand my outburst.

The story closer to our model is the "life-saving station" story. A person walking along the river hears a baby cry. The baby is floating down the river and will surely die if someone doesn't jump in and save her. So, he does. The next day, along the same river, the same person hears another baby crying in the river, and he jumps in and saves the baby. This keeps happening, and the baby rescuer recruits friends to help. Eventually, they build a station to watch for babies in the water and rescue them.

One day, a stranger comes to town and sits on the riverbank, watching the busy activity of baby saving. She asks, "Who's throwing these babies in the water?"

Friendly Planet Missiology is the stranger.

After years of being the stranger, we've made an interesting discovery. It seems that here in the Congo, a relationship has developed between those who throw the babies in the river and those who rescue them. In a super warped sort of logic, communities are throwing their babies in the river, trusting in the rescuers to be there to pull them out. Every act of charity, aid, or help reinforces this relationship, and the community comes to believe that their salvation can only be found from a foreign rescuing agency.

The problem is that there aren't enough rescuers to save all the babies, and this model is no solution at all for the long run. It completely ignores the community's own wisdom, its own assets, its own responsibility for its children. I've said this before, but it can't be said often enough. Every community possesses not just the wisdom to solve its own problems— more often than not, more often than you think, the community also possesses sufficient resources to do so.

The projects Friendly Planet Missiology ends up doing don't look any different from the projects of every other mission group or NGO. We dig wells. We build schools. We do agricultural projects to feed children. The difference is twofold. First, we actually believe that communities have the wisdom, and even the assets, to solve their problems. We hear everybody saying similar things to what we are saying. There's really not that much disagreement out there among those who are writing about development. Really. The difference is in the field, where you have to act on these beliefs. Even church-led mission programs will teach this, but when it comes to actually doing it, what people do and how they behave betrays the fact that they don't really believe what they've been saying.

To further complicate things, the people coming here to help aren't the only ones who don't believe the Congolese are smart enough to solve their problems. Over generations, the Congolese themselves have been indoctrinated into believing that they are not smart enough. A young Congolese man once said to me, "The difference between Americans and Africans is that Americans are smarter." It seems that everybody is operating out of this understanding. Observe: even education programs are built on the assumption that if the Congolese could only get smarter, they could solve these problems. I will concede the need for content education, but I counter that knowledge is not wisdom. The wisdom already exists in the community.

The second difference is that Friendly Planet takes the time to develop the leaders who will solve the problems. We don't solve the problems. They do. As a pastor, Joseph Mulongo will solve the problems. As a physician, Dr. Serge will solve the problems. As a fisherman, Éléphant will solve the problems plaguing his family and village.

Arrested in Malemba

BEFORE THE BOAT CAN begin to work the river, it will have to be registered with the Ministry of Maritime Affairs. The nearest office is in Malemba-Nkulu, a long morning ride by motorcycle. Mulongo and I take Éléphant's motorcycle; he's driving, and I'm hanging on behind.

First, we must make the early morning pirogue across the two rivers that converge at Mulongo and separate the village from its territorial capital of Malemba-Nkulu. The motorcycle is loaded onto the pirogue, and we find places for ourselves. Feeling confident and cool, I choose to sit on the gunnel. It takes the usual half-hour to cross.

Then we're off the boat and on the road, riding faster than is comfortable for me on the back, but this is transportation in the Congo. We pass through Kabwe and other familiar smaller villages that I've visited before on the bicycle. Mulongo dodges chickens, goats, and children—all seemingly unaware that they are in danger of being hit by a motorcycle. Just before we would make the turn to the right that takes the road straight up the mountain to Mwanza, we'll leave the road to take a footpath through the forest—the shortcut to Malemba-Nkulu.

Malemba-Nkulu is a good-sized town sitting on a bend in the Congo River. We enter the town through a crummy old roundabout, with a *"Bienvenue à Malemba"* sign in the center welcoming us. However, we're not made to feel that welcome—several police officers in blue man the intersection. Mulongo attempts to ignore them and go on, but they are determined not to let that happen. Mulongo says nothing and keeps looking forward as if he doesn't see them. Two officers grab the motorcycle and stop us.

"Where have you come from?"

"Where are you going?"

"What are you doing in Malemba?"

We have a problem; Éléphant's motorcycle is not registered. We have no license plate for the moto. Lacking plates is more common than having plates, especially for motorcycles and especially for motorcycles driven in remote villages. As much of a driver as Éléphant is, he doesn't have a driver's license, nor does he register any of his vehicles. It's not just the expense—it's the hassle of navigating the bureaucracy. Éléphant doesn't get along with bureaucrats.

So, Mulongo is written up for driving an unregistered motorcycle, driving an uninsured motorcycle, and driving a motorcycle without a helmet. Yes, there is a helmet law. (It must be selectively enforced.) From my American perspective, it seems strange to be fined for not wearing a helmet when they are so rarely worn here.

The problem is, now we're stuck. We've got to appeal this and at least get permission to get our business completed.

Under a shade tree by the side of the road, ignoring the whole argument, is a senior police officer getting a shave. He's too important to care. Mulongo goes over to him to plead our case, arguing not the merits of the citation but the importance of our mission. In cases like this, the mixed advantage of being white is evident. Since a white person must be an important person, my whiteness may work in our favor, and we will be cut a break.

On the other hand, there is so much repressed anger for colonial and neo-colonial oppression that a chance to stick it to a *muzungu* and his Congolese driver can be too satisfying to pass up. The senior officer refuses to entertain the problem until his shave is finished, and he isn't in a hurry with that. He continues with his shave, the barber slowly shaving not only his face but also his head.

We have a change of luck when Mulongo identifies us as pastors, United Methodist pastors. This both lightens the tension and elevates our status.

The solution: we're under arrest, but we will have to drive ourselves to the police headquarters. That we do.

We meet with the police chief, but he says that there is nothing he can do to help. He sends us to the territorial administrator. I'm hesitant to make this comparison, of course, but I'm reminded of Jesus being passed from Pilate to Herod and back again after his arrest.

The territorial administrator is more interested in talking about our work in community development and church in general. He sends us to

ANR. The intelligence and internal security agency has nothing to do with the traffic ticket, of course, but I'm a foreigner.

We head over to the ANR office, still driving ourselves. It's a routine check-in—passport, Order of Missions, questions about our work. I'm always cautious to even talk about the work, as I'm on a tourist visa. Our story is always that the church is doing the work, and I'm here to visit the work, which is God's honest truth. Having given the officer his due respect, we pass the ANR interview.

We go back to the police chief. By this time, he's in a generous mood and dismisses the charges, with stern instructions to get the motorcycle registered immediately. Throughout the whole process, Mulongo never mentioned once that the motorcycle belonged to someone else. He took all the blame without excuse.

Leaving the police headquarters, we are hit up by our arresting officer for some money. He's begging on behalf of his family. He hasn't been paid in months, and the children are starving. It's a fascinating turn in the relationship. Mulongo gives him some money.

We still have to register the boat. But first, Mulongo wants to find something to eat. He takes us to a small hotel under construction where he knows the owner. There's no restaurant open yet, but the owner invites us into his home and serves us a meal. I'm left to eat alone as Mulongo and his friend go off to talk business. I take the time to read the political posters that line the walls. I'm a guest in the home of an opposition candidate. I have no idea what that might mean, but it all feels slightly underground.

The local Minister of Maritime Affairs is ill, so we go to his home to find him. He's lying out in his paillotte on a grass mat. He clearly is not feeling well. From the looks of him, it's serious. But he welcomes our visit and greets us in a friendly manner even though he can't get up. His wife brings us drinks. This has the feel of a pastoral call. Mulongo leads in that way, and we offer a prayer for his healing.

This business is easy compared to what we've been through just to get there. The Minister has the documents we need—signed and sealed. We pay the $90 for the license to operate on the river. I ask him how many boats are registered in Malemba. Five. Wow. Friendly Planet is 20% of the commercial shipping on the Congo River out of the port of Malemba-Nkulu.

On the way back from Malemba-Nkulu to Mulongo, the trail becomes a single track in a dense section of forest, and we get off the moto and walk. Mulongo is in a talkative mood. Our adventure with the police in Malemba has brought out the storyteller in him, and I begin to learn how politically dangerous this work is for him:

> "There was a young girl who was raped by two police officers. No one would charge them with the rape, but everyone knew. As the United Methodist Superintendent, I was that girl's pastor. I had to speak for her family and for the church. I took her case to the magistrate and challenged him, 'Is this what you want our community to be, the capital of rape?' The soldiers were charged, convicted, and sent to prison. Rape is a problem in our culture. Too many men, powerful men, don't see the problem. But some men see the problem, and we have to fight for change."

Here is another piece of Friendly Planet's mission—we support the people who are supporting recovery. Since the armed conflict ended, Pastor Jacqueline Ngoy Mwayuma has been in ministry with the war's rape survivors. Their needs are great, but the Gospel that Jackie carries is greater. And she can do this good work because she knows we're there with her. Because it can be lonely doing difficult work in remote areas, we're taking this journey to visit Pastor Jackie to confirm our commitment to her ministry, so she knows we haven't forgotten her, so she knows that we still value her work. The message of Friendly Planet is getting simpler. We have friends in faraway places, doing incredible ministry, who count on our friendship. That's it.

Trying to Explain the Mission of Friendly Planet Missiology

SHABANA WRITES:

On our 2010 tour, while we were climbing the mount *Kana ka kisonsa* [the Mother of all Mountains], Bob sat down to rest for a while. In a whispering voice, he told me, "Shabana, I can see the suffering of these communities," and he paused before continuing, "something must be done."

"Surely," I replied, "something should be done." This is the expression that pushed me much to try to understand what was Baba Bob's mission that we all did not understand.

Most of the people we met asked me the same question to which I did not have a right answer. We heard questions like these: What has Bob come for? Why does he prefer to come on a bicycle? Is it that he does not have enough means for you to come in a car? Should we hope to find a solution to the problems we have, or is he a *mzungu mulanda* [white servant] who himself rides a bicycle to come towards where we are?

It was difficult for me to answer such questions, and I just said, "Well, he has good projects for these remote areas, and he is using the bicycle to better understand your real problems." My answer satisfied neither the people nor myself because even by using another kind of transport, one could always understand the real problem.

In this conversation with Baba Bob, I realized it was also important for me to better know his great concern for these communities and why he was using the bicycle to reach them.

Baba Bob then answered me, saying, "Shabana, we are trying to do something quite different from the other missionaries, but which will attract everybody's attention. For with planes, cars, motorbikes, we will be able to attract neither Congolese people's

Trying to Explain the Mission

attention nor those from abroad. Also, we have been fundraising and distributing bicycles to pastors; we have, therefore, to show them that a bicycle is a better means of transport since it does not require fuel, a driver's license, or other documents to give to the police and other administrations. So it is an excellent way to travel, especially on bad roads where trucks get stuck but a bicycle just passes through."

With this answer, I tried to understand Baba Bob and his Friendly Planet Missiology. By its motto—"small footprint, big change"—it is clear that Baba Bob was trying to work with a kind of psychological change in the way the mission is done and understood in our communities.

Bob wanted to change the perception in our mind that a missionary should be a patron by trying to create a mission of proximity, a mission that is not supposed to be different from the communities it is appointed to, a mission which does not appear to be a sort of patron or boss.

Previous missionaries had used bicycles only as hobbies with their families in their houses, but Baba Bob used it as a means of transport towards these remote communities. Missionaries took with them food, water, mattress, but Baba Bob ate the food locally cooked everywhere he arrived with love and desire, drinking the local DRC water, and slept on our beds, in every sort of house, not wanting just to stay at special hotels or guesthouses.

Bob has followed the example of Jesus, coming from the glory of his father to the lowest place on earth. Staying and eating with the people who were considered the scum of the Jewish society. Bob started by involving himself in Congolese society to better see things as they do, and so it should be easier to understand their real problems and together set up a plan of help. Baba Bob was convinced, as I am, that the problem of poverty in much of the poor communities is not only the lack of money but that the problem was still in the mind.

First and foremost, his act of using a bicycle has been a way of telling to the church leaders and all the people in my communities that there was no excuse not to get to such remote areas. He wanted to tell people that the problem is also that we don't accept delay; therefore, we cannot even accomplish any project. People just want to leave Lubumbashi today and get to Mulongo the same day, but with a bicycle, it can take them four days. Therefore, if they cannot afford the cost of a flight, they will accept to quit the plan rather than to use the bicycle for four days and still carry out their project.

While building a church, people want to start today and finish tomorrow, yet we can build a church by starting with the rocks one year, bricks the next year, and so on until we finish, even if it can take a decade. Baba Bob wanted to show people that being a missionary is to live as a member of the community you are assigned to. Mission is not to provide with cloth, money, and medicine, but to be part of the community, to create a participative leadership, a kind of leadership where every member of the community participates, including the missionary. Baba Bob also wanted to show to our church leaders that the work of developing our communities was not to be left only to the missionaries. It is not just with money that we should visit the remote communities.

Bob has demonstrated a real love for being present in the places that most of the church leaders have never been. They make so many excuses: there are no good roads to get to those areas, it is not safe for us to cross through the *Triangle de la Mort*, there are not comfortable hotels or guesthouses to stay in, there is neither food nor pure water for such or such category of people. Yet Bob from the U. S. was able to sleep in local houses, to eat the local food, and to use the local water both for drinking and washing.

Joseph concurs with Shabana's assessment, writing:

Just after meeting Bob at General Conference in 2008, I was interested to join him on the first tour he planned on the bicycle because I saw in him someone who was very passionate in mission and especially someone who loved North Katanga. It was just after the war, and no missionaries had been visiting North Katanga. The people had been abandoned by the church leadership because nobody could visit them. Everybody was afraid of being killed. Everybody was afraid because there was no clean water, no good sanitation systems. But Bob decided to go. I know that people had been telling him, "There is no road. There is no good water. Everything is bad." When he arrived in Lubumbashi in 2010, he said, "Joseph, I was told that there was no good water; that's why I brought a filter. They said there are no good houses, that there are bugs in the houses; that's why I brought my tent. I can spend the night in the tent. There is no road; that's why I would like to ride my bicycle."

We started the first ride in Tenke. From Tenke to Mulongo and back to Tenke, crossing what we call the Triangle of Death, Bob was bringing hope to people. His arrival in villages that had been abandoned for so many years brought hope. We were received under the rain when we arrived in Kasengeshi, one of the villages. It was raining, and the people came from different corners to welcome Bob. They said, "He is the only one who has recognized that there are people somewhere. We know that the church exists. We did not know that we are known somewhere by somebody because all the missionaries from different congregations, from different denominations, have left." At that time, Bob was the first missionary to arrive. He was the first white person. People had been seeing white people from the UN, who were escorted by armies for their security, but people were surprised to see a white person coming on a bicycle, so he was a symbol of hope. Bob brought a new spirit to the abandoned church. He came to visit people recovering from a war.

To Kabalo

The next day, the boat is loaded, and we push off for Kabalo. First stop: Kabumbulo. It's a cluster of villages along the Congo River. Each village has a chief, but the chiefs meet together under the Chef de Groupement, the chief of the village group.

Here is where we catch up with the beginning of this volume: on a boat, on the Congo River, tied up for the night at the village of Kabumbulo, reading *Heart of Darkness*, reflecting on a journey now into its second year and finally on our way to Kabalo, our original destination. We'll be there tomorrow. Here is where the writing of this book began.

Joseph says to me, "Everything you have heard about the war, it happened here." He left it at that. Nothing more needed to be said.

Our arrival here—at a district we could not visit on our first bicycle tour, at a place that has had so much impact from the war—feels momentous to me. But we have work to do.

The crew offloads the 110 sheets of roofing that we have been carrying on the top of the *Indiana's* canopy. The canopy's construction makes for a perfect lumber and sheet metal rack for hauling. Local men carry the sheets of tin up the hill. These roofing sheets have been purchased by Dr. Ivan for the clinic he is building here.

We go to see the clinic under construction. There's been a mission clinic here since the 1920s, and we pass the old British Brethren clinic that the new one is replacing. The old clinic has a classic colonial look, very Belgian. It also has one huge gaping crack running more or less diagonally top to bottom on the major exterior wall. It appears to have been the victim of an earthquake, but it is actually just giving way to years of rain. The building is settling as the ground underneath it washes away. I love these old buildings, but they are finished.

The new clinic is rather plain compared to the building it is replacing. Dr. Ivan's vision is a series of small village clinics connected in a hub and spoke system with the British Brethren hospital in Mulongo. The village clinics will be staffed by nurses trained at the El Dorado Nursing School in Mulongo. (Friendly Planet helped to build El Dorado and provides scholarships for students to attend.) We encounter one of the best characteristics of United Methodists in North Katanga: we are committed to working with others. We partner with other Christian denominations, government and non-government agencies, even Muslims and those practicing traditional Bantu beliefs. We drill this commitment into our pastors and lay leaders, and brag about it to donors. It is a genuine commitment. We believe in it both theologically and as a strategy for community development.

This commitment seems to confuse the folks back home. I'm always caught off guard when someone in a church in Indiana asks me if there are Muslims in the villages where we work or if we get any resistance to evangelism. These questions are fishing for a juicy story of Christian persecution.

Now, I need to explain that my observations and the missiological conclusions I reach are specific to this particular place, time, and people. My observations and conclusions are not about Cambodia, where Christians are a tiny minority, and Christian missionaries must adhere to tight restrictions on their work as set out by the Ministry of Cult and Religion. (I have visited with United Methodist missionaries in Cambodia and have been impressed by the humility of their Christian witness in a land where they are guests.) Neither are my observations about Sudan, where warring factions are identified as Christian or Muslim. Nominally, just about everyone in Congo is a Christian, and, on top of that, in North Katanga, the United Methodists number over one million. For me, the biggest question about evangelism remains: has all this evangelism helped the people in their daily lives? I'm not so sure.

United Methodists' commitment to working with others is not necessarily understood well by those we want to partner with in Congo, either. The clinic in Kabumbalo is a test case for our being able to partner with a group that is not committed to the same set of development rules we are. But we're caught in a labor dispute. The laborers want us to hear their grievances against the local British Brethren Congolese pastor in charge of the project. This is where it gets sticky. Our connection to this building project is through Dr. Ivan, and only in a big picture way. This is not our project. In support of the construction, we are simply delivering roofing.

The sticky part is that the pastor is not holding up his end of the deal with the construction workers. The local British Brethren church members are supposed to be providing food for the workers. The workers, however, have not only not been paid, but they're also not even being fed. So, we get a tour of the construction site by the lead builder, who is proud to show off their progress. Then, we sit down to a labor negotiation. Joseph handles our side of the talks, basically trying to stay out of the direct conflict but affirming the deal that the local Brethren congregation has to provide food.

Afterward, he confides in me that this pastor is doing a poor job of leadership and is costing the project dearly. That pastor does not understand what we, as a team, are trying to accomplish. He is only interested in what he can get out of the deal. He thinks he is some kind of "chief." This is not the first time Joseph Mulongo has let me know how difficult it is to work with British Brethren here. They just don't get what we get. They don't have our vision. But we have to find a way to work with the British Brethren. The hospital in Mulongo is a British Brethren mission hospital. It's supported by Irish missionaries, though we don't seem to visit during the same months, so I've never met them.

A note to the reader: I realize that I criticize our British Brethren partners more harshly than I criticize United Methodists. I feel a bit sheepish, since I've learned that some British Brethren have read *The Last Missionary*. My criticism still stands, but I could be nicer to the Brethren. Or stop being so nice to the Methodists.

The Snake House

We walk through one village and toward another in this string of villages along the river. The crowd is growing, and there are hundreds of children. The crowd makes space for a 12-year-old boy to approach me to share something special. His name is Bob. Robert is a common enough name, but as far as I know, I'm the only Bob that has ever been in this area. His age means that he was born when I was a missionary in the Lubudi and Mitwaba Districts. Let me be clear: he's not my son. But it's pretty likely that his mother named him after me, and that's a strange feeling.

The dirt road we're on intersects a smaller, one-track foot trail, decorated with a traditional hoop of palm branches and flowers over the entrance. These hoops last only a day or two, so I know it was put up today just to welcome us. An old brick house stands at the end of the trail. As with many other colonial-era houses, the ground has washed away around it, and stepping up to the first step of the front veranda is a challenge. A large unstable stone makes for a temporary fix to the problem, and I rock on it as I step up. Turning around, I'm facing one of the biggest crowds of our trip. We exchange formal greetings.

The house had been abandoned for years during the war. When the property owner sent his brother to the village to reclaim the house, the jungle had already claimed it. The vegetation was cleared, and the house cleaned, but the snakes who had taken up residence persisted long enough to create the nickname Snake House. Now you know why Congolese homes don't have grass yards. Conscientious homeowners sweep their dirt yards every day to ensure that snakes do not return.

Which reminds me: have I told you my snake story?

On the 1998 ride through the Lubudi District, we rode along a mountain ridge. I stopped to look at a large black snake coiled on the side of the trail. Everyone else hustled by.

At the time, my Swahili wasn't bad, and I could ask basic questions. So I did: "What is this?"

"It's a snake."

"I know it's a snake. What do you call it?"

"A snake."

I didn't know the word for venomous or poisonous, but I knew the word for dangerous. "Is it dangerous?"

"Yes. It's a snake."

So, here's hoping that the snakes have moved on from the Snake House.

My bedroom is the master bedroom of the house. The bed is actually large and netted, and the Homer Simpson sheets make me smile. I pull the mosquito net around the bed, settle in, read a bit on my Nook, and go to sleep.

Kabumbulu

THE CHIEF OF THE GROUP of villages that makes up Kabumbulu has asked us to stop by for a chat. This is a serious request that we take seriously. As with any visit to a chief, we know this meeting will start later than scheduled and take longer than planned. Our desire to get going early in the day has been trumped by the chief's request.

Our team shows up at the appointed time. The chief isn't even present, but we remove our caps as we enter his yard anyway. This is about the only protocol that I have run into that seems to be inviolate. Every other cultural *faux pas* seems to be overlooked or quickly forgiven, but not removing your hat in the chief's yard causes great consternation for everyone present. The chief will be the only one wearing a hat within the fenced area that defines the yard, and usually, it will be a leopard-print, straw cowboy hat.

Hats off, we seat ourselves in a circle in the yard and settle in to wait. As the chief comes out of his house, it's fascinating to watch his transition from a family man having breakfast with his wife and children to the head of all the villages along a ten-kilometer stretch of river. He's in a suit, not a great suit, but a business suit nonetheless. No tie, though. And no hat. And he's young for a chief.

This chief is not the old sort of traditional chief, the more-show-than-go sort. This chief is more than a traditional chief. All the other chiefs of this group of villages have elected him chief of the chiefs, and he takes his job seriously. He is clearly highly educated and talks with us about development. He walks a line between asking for our help and letting us know that he is the one doing the development. He's proud, he's smart, and he knows his clout. He is the Big Man.

This chief is a perfect example of the new generation of village leaders. Having gone to Lubumbashi for their education, these leaders now have houses there and return to their respective villages just enough to reinforce their status and control. These chiefs are both the solution and the problem. Many are skilled in using the existing broken, corrupt system to get the things their villages need and feather their own nests. They are the rich among the very poor.

This chief is among the best, and his words are spot on. He has a clear understanding of what the community needs. I can imagine how our small non-profit could help this one chief transform this group of villages, but there is no way we could do much more than one such group of villages, and there are thousands of these villages. We don't have the capacity to do what needs to be done, even if what we could do would be a real solution.

No matter how well these chiefs work the system, the villages are always still going to be poor. There's enough help coming to feed the belief that more help is coming. There's enough development done to create a hope that more development is coming. But it's not coming. Not any time soon. This system will never deliver enough outside help to get the villages out of their poverty, only enough to get them through the next year or the next day. No agency, church, or government program will provide enough help to break the cycle. And the big NGOs are not helping at all. Their help is only delaying the end and creating hope in a kind of help that will not be helpful in the long run. In villages like this one, we see an occasional water project, a sanitary toilet project, or a partially finished school. But we never see a project that has both been finished and is delivering the promised change for the people.

After the audience with the chief, we take the long walk back to our boat. It has, in fact, been moved to another village. We walk through a complex built for training in agriculture, cotton milling, and animal husbandry. It clearly cost a lot to build this complex, but the mission it was meant to serve lasted less than five years before it was abandoned. This complex was the project of a progressive woman, a Presbyterian missionary who was far from the center of Presbyterian missions in central Congo.

The cause of its abandonment was a political fight between the American Presbyterians who were funding the mission and the Congolese Presbyterian pastor. He had been elected as the leader of the provincial Presbyterian church. He took this to be an election to permanent ownership of the denomination's property, which had all been registered in his name. Although he now lives in Lubumbashi, he still claims personal ownership of the property, and the missionary has gone home.

Kabumbulu

As I looked over this failed project, I could see how with just a few tweaks of the model, it could have worked. Congo was once famous for its cotton, so I'm especially intrigued by the possibility of restarting cotton farming in this area. Before there was the world-famous Egyptian cotton, there was Congolese cotton. Even in Zambia today, people choose Congolese cotton over Zambian. Along the river, we have seen the old cotton warehouses in ruin. The textile industry that was once huge here could be again. If I were Cecil Rhodes and came to the Congo, I'd grow cotton.

Arrival in Kabalo

WE'RE MAKING OUR WAY UPRIVER. Correction, downriver. The Congo River makes a wide circle around the DRC, going north from Katanga, swinging west in the northern provinces, then south to Kinshasa and the Atlantic Ocean. Here, it's flowing north. My navigational confusion is that north on the map is up for me, but on the river, up is against the current. So, we are going north, downriver to Kabalo.

It's midday under a sunny blue sky. At a wide spot in the river, we pass some old cotton warehouses and shipping stations up high on the bank. They probably weren't in good shape before the war, and now they're just shells. The roofs have been bombed off or stripped for their metal.

Up ahead, the only bridge that crosses the Congo River for 500 kilometers comes into view. It's a combination rail and road bridge; not a rail and road bridge, as in two-level, or side by side, but the road and the rail are the same, one-lane bridge. It's long enough that if you're going to cross by truck, you'd better be certain that there is no train coming. It's actually not that big a problem, though. The train crosses here once a week at best. It's more like once a month, or even months between trains. When it does run, it connects Kamina and Kalemie.

Whether on the Ohio, the Mississippi, or the Congo, passing under a bridge on a river is cool. A half-hour after we've first sighted the bridge, we cross under it. This bridge is a marvel of European engineering, built by African sweat almost 100 years ago to extend colonial expansion. I can only imagine where the steel came from. Sheffield? One of the puzzles of the redevelopment of this region is that there are still people old enough to remember when these bridges and railroads connected the deepest parts of Africa with Europe. It didn't benefit the local population in significant ways, but the loss of this connection is deeply felt. Taylor tells a story about working with one of those people old enough to remember. In 2005, it was

Arrival in Kabalo

difficult to get basic office supplies in Kamina, but Taylor's coworker recounted the days when one could order supplies from a catalog by telegram and receive them by train within days.

This bridge was a key strategic objective in the war, as bridges tend to be. I'm surprised that it wasn't blown up. But that might have taken more explosives than one might think. Any rational military commander would want this bridge intact after taking it, but the military commanders in this war were not always rational. A suspicious person might wonder if the sanctity of this bridge indicates that there was a commercial objective more powerful than any military objective that drove this war. The flow of gold and coltan trumped any political agenda.

About five kilometers after the bridge, we see Kabalo. There is a rail station with a water tower for the old steam engines and a port for the big riverboats that used to come here, but we pass all that to pull into a shallow beach and park with the fishing pirogues.

The Kabalo District of The United Methodist Church shows up in force for a formal welcome. Hundreds of school children in ranks and files, by school, with banners identifying their school and welcoming the visitors, form a square around the "parade" field. United Methodist Women with colorful dresses and large parasols sing and dance the welcome. District Superintendent Jacqueline Mwayuma, the person we have come all this way to visit, accompanied by the district lay leader and the clergy elders, greets us with the protocol of a welcome to a bishop or a governor. When she and I hug, I feel like we are making a historical moment, a "Dr. Livingstone, I presume" moment. If anything ever comes of these adventures, this moment defines it. We have arrived in Kabalo—the city destroyed in the war, the city abandoned and forgotten. When Friendly Planet and the Methodist Church manage to bring real help up here, this will have been the moment it began. If my life has ever accomplished anything, this is the moment.

There's another official at the boat to greet us, but we pretty much ignore him. He's in uniform, accompanied by two police officers. With a big grin, I shake his hand as if he were one of the many dignitaries who showed up to meet the boat. Mulongo ignores him at first—I figure out later—in order to ignore the fact that he has come for immigration matters. Eventually, Mulongo informs him that we'll report to immigration tomorrow.

We get into the parade that the church has organized—marching and singing and dancing into town. Scouts are guarding the way, and United Methodist Women, with their bright parasols, give the parade both music and the look of a colorful community festivity. It's sunny, and it's hot. Sunnier and hotter than any other place we've been—this is a new level of burning heat. Even the sun teaches us how scorched this town is.

The parade ends at the site of the United Methodist church building, which is under construction. Under Jackie's leadership, the church is rebuilding after its destruction in the war. Typical of such reconstruction projects, the local congregation has made and fired the bricks and put up the walls. The timbers for the roof are still stacked on the ground, already formed into rafters. Without the cash for cement and roofing, the church is stuck. Even if they had the cash, getting cement and roofing to Kabalo would be difficult. Transport challenges mean a five-dollar bag of cement would cost $50 in Kabalo—if it were available at all.

Jackie

JACKIE NGOY MWAYUMA WAS SENT to the Kabalo District as the first woman district superintendent in the Tanganyika Conference. Her appointment by the Bishop was quite intentional. Jackie was trained in post-trauma counseling at Africa University in Zimbabwe, and the issues in Kabalo are all women's issues. Her job is to lead this district in rebuilding community. It was our job to let her know that she was not doing this alone. By taking the *UM Indiana* to Kabalo, we have opened up the Tanganyika Conference to the flow of communication and assistance. She will no longer be isolated but fully connected.

Kabalo is a railhead for the train coming from Kalemie. Goods from Tanganyika come by boat to the port in Kalemie and are put on the train heading west to the interior. At Kabalo, the goods can continue west or be distributed by boat on the Congo River. Kabalo commands the only bridge over the river for several hundred kilometers north or south. During the war, it was important to hold Kabalo, and it was overrun four times. The armies from Rwanda and Uganda occupied the east side of the bridge, while the armies of Zimbabwe and the DRC occupied the west side.

The biggest recovery issue concerns rape, and rape comes in several forms. There was rape that was used as a weapon of war: women were publicly and violently raped in front of their fathers and brothers. It may seem that "violently" is an unnecessary modifier for the word "rape," but the violence here was meant to be so horrific as to terrorize the community beyond imagination. The men of the family and of the village were shamed to the point of immobility. I don't wish to divide acts of rape into categories of relative violence, but I want you to know that this violence against women, young women, and little girls was brutal to the point of removing a village's ability to fight back. Any men who attempted to come to the defense of the women were chopped up by machete. Every act was, by design, a brutal and visually terrifying act.

Public rape was not the only rape. Soldiers of visiting armies took "wives" for themselves during the occupation, including girls as young as thirteen. These girls were raped by their captors, and they had to serve them by cooking for them and doing their laundry. Then, when that army moved on, these child wives were left behind with the children they had borne.

Kabalo became a town of women left behind by the war. The men of combat age had gone off to fight or had been killed defending the village. This was the district to which Jackie was appointed. Her task has been to provide leadership to a community of women recovering from rape and raising the children of rape.

Jackie has done an incredible job leading this district back from complete destruction. I once watched her work in Kalemie during an annual conference session. The Bishop had put her in charge of the cabinet meeting while he tended to a local conflict. She was skilled in leading that group of men; they clearly respected her leadership.

But Jackie is now stuck. She's brought the district as far as she can without resources from the broader church, and she needs some help. I have brought five one-hundred-dollar bills in an envelope from Denver Thornton, her friend in Arkansas who prodded me into making this trip, but that money is a gift for her personal and family needs. The reconstruction of the Kabalo District is going to need thousands of dollars.

My passion begins to burn, and I ask the question, "Where is The United Methodist Church? Where is the General Board of Global Ministries? Where is UMCOR (the United Methodist Committee on Relief)?" We have traveled to the farthest outpost of The United Methodist Church and find a church that has been abandoned and forgotten. I'm here, but I'm freelancing. Where are the official representatives of the UMC? We've taken nearly five years, by bicycle and in a locally-built boat, to get here. Where are the others, the ones who are supposed to respond to these sorts of disasters?

If this book has a message, it is this: Where was The United Methodist Church when these colleagues needed help? And why don't we have money and people in here now to help out? We go all over the world in response to war and natural disasters; why aren't we here? These are our people, but we have abandoned them.

Too strong? I don't think so.

Unfair? No.

Faith, Comfort, and Friendship

JACKIE WRITES:

I first met Baba Bob at General Conference in the US in 2008. I was asked to talk about my district and its social and spiritual situation. It was after the war, and I had been appointed as the first female superintendent in the Kabalo District. I didn't realize who would be touched by that story.

I had been feeling abandoned. As a woman, it was dangerous coming to a devastated area, a post-conflict zone. Security was not assured for me as many women were being sexually abused and were victims of violence. I complained to the Bishop. I had to visit different locations 50–90 km from Kabalo. It was not easy for me to go alone into the bush.

After my presentation, one of the people waved a hand to ask a question. He asked me, "Since the Bishop sent you to Kabalo, where everything has been devastated by the war, have you received any support?" I responded, "No, I haven't received any support, supplies, or funds to rebuild the infrastructure destroyed by the civil war." That was Bob. When I finished that presentation, I had no idea how deeply he had been affected by my explanation.

Bob didn't say anything to me about visiting. But Bob had decided to come to see the reality I described in my presentation.

I was very surprised and excited when he showed up two years later. We were all amazed by the determination and faith it took to make the trip to an inaccessible zone—cycling to Mulongo, then on a small boat, practically a canoe, through the Kabalo district. It was so amazing to see Bob and this FPM team of servants of God when they reached Kabalo in a canoe. We could see Baba Bob was faithful, passionate, ready to share the good news. I could see in him Matthew 11:28-29 that he had been given a mission to go preach the gospel to those who are very far.

When we saw him coming, cycling, embarking on the boat, and reaching this area with no facilities, no infrastructure, we realized we could learn a lot. It was so amazing to see this big team of servants of God coming to us. I could read through his face someone who was very passionate with the kind of love he has for people. I could read in Baba Bob, a person who has committed to achieving his goal. He had very high endurance. There were many challenges on his path, and he was giving up everything to meet his goal.

I could also see Bob as a servant who was engaged and available for needy people. He would listen and try to understand each person at their own level. He spent all his time listening and paying attention to what others thought about their ministry. He would comfort as much as he could. He was a servant who also enabled other servants. When he passed away, no one could believe he could have died.

It was like when Abraham had three angels come to visit his house. Bob and the FPM team brought the blessing of those angels visiting my house. They were staying together with us and eating together with us. He was very patient, listening carefully to everyone. There was still no good road or infrastructure because of the lack of resources since the war. Because the district didn't have enough resources to develop spiritually and socially, he was one who was willing to support us in every way. Bob could choose to go anywhere else but chose our Kabalo district. Through that visit, Baba Bob and FPM approved four projects in Kabalo. He promised that, God willing, he would work on raising money for:

1. the district superintendent's house, so the servant of God could find a safe place to stay during ministry;
2. a guest house for the Kabalo District;
3. a boat for transportation of goods from Kabalo to Kongolo on the Congo River to help generate income for the district pastors and needy people
4. a memorial church for everyone to see

He also supported my work with the Foyer in Kabalo. Because of the culture and customs, people were giving education more to men than women, so we as the church had been working hard to make the point understood that they should not give more privileges to men than women. We had been trying to help women to read and write, especially the Bible and its contents. These ladies should be taught to learn different activities to allow them to be

Faith, Comfort, and Friendship

independent, provide for their families, and support the work of the church. Even without the building, I was working with these women. My hope was that if the community center were built, more ladies would be coming and learning.

There is a proverb that a very good friend is seen during troubles. They come and comfort you. The visit of Bob and the Friendly Planet team comforted everyone and brought hope to everyone. Someone was praying and supporting and loving us.

Preaching in Kabalo

On the second day in Kabalo, we drop by the office of the territorial administrator to check in. He's not in his office. We go on about our business. Jackie takes us on a tour of what used to be the flagship church of the Kabalo District. What we find is only a footprint of the district parsonage. We can see where the front steps used to be. That's all that's left of them. The parsonage for the pastor and his family is only half standing—one side wall gone, grass roof falling in on the home. The church is not half bad, I think. Not great, but it does have walls and a grass roof. Mumba is in tears. This was his home church. It was here he received his call to ministry. It was here he started out as a youth pastor. He tells me of the large, beautiful church that used to be here. He points me to the place in the bush where a house once stood, the house he lived in. This is a sad day for him.

There is some good news. World Vision has been here and rebuilt half of the school, and it's in good shape. World Vision works closely with United Methodists. In fact, when World Vision first came to the area, they operated under the United Methodist Church's auspices until they received their own status as an NGO. Many of the buildings that house United Methodist schools and clinics were built by World Vision. In this part of the world, they take on the responsibilities for construction, leaving programming to others.

After our tours of the church and school, we still haven't made contact with the district administrator. Mulongo goes to see him solo, sensing that I should not be in the room. The administrator is not happy that we're here. He wants to know why I'm traveling on a tourist visa and not a missionary visa. Mulongo is great in these meetings. He stands toe to toe with high-ranking politicians and seldom has to pay any kind of bribe. He says, "Fine, we'll leave. You tell the people why you ran us off." We are allowed to stay.

Preaching in Kabalo

Sunday comes, and I preach. The district administrator—who is not a United Methodist—is in the front row. He never cracks a smile. The youth do a skit that tries to get audience participation. The administrator ignores the youth and just sits there.

The sermon was our stock, "I know of your poverty, but you are rich," speech. I was unaware that my invitation in the sermon to take advantage of rich farmland was not helpful in a district where landmines filled the fields. During the war, invading armies had been in the area long enough to completely seed all the farmers' fields with landmines. The congregation responded to my sermon with, "but the fields are still dangerous with mines"—something I hadn't considered. I should have picked up on that earlier when we had stopped the boat along the river to take a pee and were met with signs warning us to stay on the path. And then there were all the Danish trucks in town with land mine removal signs on their doors.

After church, there was a lunch at the home where we were staying. This house was unusual in that it was still standing. I asked and had it confirmed for me: the house had remained untouched because this was the house generals stayed in when occupying Kabalo. This was the headquarters of the war.

Anyway, there was lunch. All the pastors of town, from every denomination, were invited. The district administrator was also invited. Awkward.

But wait, it gets better. As we all discussed the sermon, the president of the ministerial association—not a United Methodist—said, "The answer to our problems is prayer. We must pray to God and wait for God to answer." The district administrator ripped into him. "You preachers always say that. It's not time to pray and wait. It's time to work!" He and I, in that instant, became co-conspirators against the preachers who preach "pray and wait." From that moment on, I was determined to use this division between the "pray and wait" preachers and the "roll up your sleeves and get to work" preachers.

When I finally did get an audience with the administrator, it turned into a delightful exchange of ideas. I learned that his bias against visiting do-gooders was well-founded. He had just thrown out a foreign NGO that was there to develop a local community mining group and whose project ended badly. I had to prove to him that I wasn't like them.

When we went to see the ANR officer, he lectured us on why I should get a missionary visa. I humbly received his advice and said that the next time I would request one, but in my defense, the embassy in Washington,

D.C. doesn't offer it. (I try to work "Washington, D.C.," into the conversation as often as possible without implying that I have any political authority.)

Cycling around Kabalo

JACKIE TAKES US ON a day trip to tour the district. We get the bicycles out of the boat; Jackie rides a motorcycle. We ride down to the bridge.

On this ride, I first notice a creaking sound that concerns me because it sounds like I might have a cracked frame on my bicycle. Also, on this ride, I finally hit a child in a village. It was bound to happen, and it did. A small boy turned right into me, looking at another bike. He more ran into me than I ran into him. No harm done.

At the bridge, we stop for a briefing on the war, the importance of the bridge, and the fate of the villages on either side. During the war, armies from Rwanda and Uganda came from the northeast and occupied Kabalo. Armies from Angola, Zimbabwe, and the Congo came from the west to take back the bridge. This was not a local civil war; it was a pan-African war.

The villages on either side of the bridge were burned to the ground four different times. Women were raped at every turn of the war. No side was guiltless.

We had time to visit two villages. We worshiped in their half-rebuilt churches. In one village, we were introduced to the chief—a woman—and a good friend of Jackie's. I am again amazed at the resilience of the women in this region. One on hand, it was the women who suffered the violence of this war. On the other hand, it is the women who are leading the community in its recovery.

Foyer

BACK IN KABALO, Jackie takes us to the meeting of her foyer group.

A foyer is a tradition introduced by old-school missionaries. Those missionaries came in couples, the husband being the primary missionary, a preacher, or a doctor, with the wife trailing with the children. The missionary wife would set up a Bible study for the women in the foyer of the missionaries' home. There, reading and writing, along with homemaking skills, would be taught. The idea of an informal school for women has continued in the church.

Jackie has set up a foyer for the women of Kabalo; no entryway to the missionary's house is involved. This "foyer" is embodied by the group of women. Often they meet in the church with no roof, sitting in the corner that has the shade. Someday they will have a separate building. The foyer is for those who could not go to school because of the war or simply because they were girls who weren't sent to school. Especially, it is for those women whose lives had been torn apart by the war. Jackie gathered rape victims, women who had been taken as wives by visiting soldiers, and women who were raising children conceived in rape and kidnapping. The women gather to learn sewing and knitting, to learn to read the Bible, to learn child care, but mostly to learn that someone cares about their lives and their futures.

When we meet with these women, they are surprisingly open about telling us their stories. We film some interviews. Maybe we'll post them somewhere eventually. Or maybe not.

Jackie has created this school, like she has done everything else here, with no help from outside. Two women of the community volunteer their time to teach sewing and knitting. Maybe sewing and knitting aren't the most important skills to learn, but those are the skills offered by the women who have volunteered to teach. The hope is that the women learning to sew can sell what they make to earn some income. I doubt that will work out, but you start where you are with what you have.

If there were just one project that I had to put everything into, it would be this foyer. The righteous cause of these women demands the investment, and besides, it would do more long-term good for the community than just about anything else. The recovery of this community from the war is ultimately tied to these women's recovery.

The recovery of these women from the war is ultimately tied up with making these communities safe again. The women cannot be whole—no one can be whole—if the threats are still out there. And they are. The warlords still control villages in the region. We decide to visit one on our way back.

Nvwendee's Village

The Mai-Mai warlord Nvwendee was not at home when we came north from Mulongo to Kabalo, but there's a rumor that he is in his village now. Joseph is determined to stop on our way back and make a pastoral call. It takes a whole day to get there.

At midday, we pass Ankora, which is a mystery to me. There is a large and, from a distance, beautiful Catholic monastery on the rise overlooking the riverfront. There is also some sort of multistory government building. Uniformed troops fill the parade ground. A huge Congolese flag is flying on the towering flagpole. The riverfront is protected with security lights, each with its own solar panel for power. The whole scene seems to be out of place—it's too big and too fancy for this remote location on the river. A lot of new money has gone into an ancient facility in a far-off place on the bend in the Congo River. If you've ever seen *The African Queen*, you've already seen this place: it's the fortress commanding the river.

We swing wide. I don't think there's any danger of being shot at, but the less attention we draw to our little boat, the better. I'm thinking that if the Bishop wanted me stationed in the Tanganyika Conference, Ankora would be the place to be. But we're not going to stop to look around.

By the time we get to Nvwendee's village, it's getting late, but it's not dark yet. We come ashore and are greeted warmly by his people. Nvwendee's people tell us that he is still out fishing and will be back after sunset, and he wants us to wait for him. We wait.

Chairs are brought, and I am given the good plastic one. There are also a couple cracked plastic ones, a couple homemade bamboo chairs, and a kitchen chair. A woman in blue jeans joins us. She pulls up a metal stool and leans into the circle. She is in charge. The rest of the adults give her the best place. The children, on the other hand, hang around her.

Nvwendee's Village

She starts talking to our team. Of course, I don't know what she is saying, but I know that she is saying it well. This is the most poised, eloquent, self-confident, and gracious lady I have met on the trip. And that includes all the terrific women leaders we met in Kabalo. Even though I can't understand her words, I'm mesmerized by her storytelling. Her hands and her face say so much.

I look closely at her necklace. The Mai-Mai are known for their necklaces of human body parts, including genitalia. Her simple necklace is made of shells.

Word comes that Nvwendee is on his way, so we move toward his camp. On the way, Mulongo fills me in that this woman is Nvwendee's niece and second in command. Her name is Masangu Charlotte, but some people call her Chatty. Many know her simply as "the Shooter." My drive to support women in leadership overrides my concern about her violent history. You don't get to be Number 2 in the camp of a warlord by playing nice. And you don't get the nickname of the Shooter at the county fair. I know all of that, but the stories about Chatty don't match what I'm reading in her face and body language right now.

Joseph Mulongo has been making pastoral calls on the warlord Nvwendee for several years now. Nvwendee hasn't changed his ways or beliefs, and he hasn't come to church personally, but the visits have had an impact on the community.

Between our 2011 visit to their village and the writing of this book, Nvwendee's daughter enrolled in the nursing school in Mulongo. This was not easy for her, the faculty, or the other students. When she got angry or frustrated, she would become violent and irrational, putting others in mortal danger. A psychiatrist might say she was suffering from severe PTSD; I can only guess at the traumas she'd experienced. She was disciplined by the school and sent home. She begged to be re-enrolled and was given a second chance. It took a lot of leadership on Mulongo's part to convince the faculty and other students to accept her back. It took a lot of patience and toughness for the community to provide the kind of pastoral care she needed in order to love the wild rage out of her.

In March 2013, two years after this 2011 meeting on the river, 600 Mai-Mai came into Lubumbashi to surrender to the UN. Despite my knowledge of the atrocities they had committed, all I could see was a sad group of defeated people. I could only pity them. I shared my feelings with Mulongo and found that he felt the same. Unfortunately, the government troops did not share our pity. When the Mai-Mai marched into Lubumbashi, government troops shot them down in the street before they could reach the UN compound. Dozens were killed.

This is so morally complex. Why should I pity rapists? Why should I have compassion for those who have shown no compassion? Why should I feel anything for those who have reigned terror on the villages I've been visiting? Maybe because I'm not sure that the story I've been told about them is entirely the truth. Maybe the Mai-Mai have been scapegoated for the atrocities committed by government soldiers and the rebel armies coming over from Rwanda and Uganda. Maybe it's because, even if they are guilty of these crimes, I've seen brave pastors like Joseph Mulongo engage in the long hard work of preaching peace in a violent environment. Maybe it's because I've seen the fear behind the violence. Maybe it's because I've been invited into their homes.

When Nvwendee arrives at this meeting in 2011, it's very late, and it's very dark. We're outside in a rather large compound of modest huts. Nothing here is fancy, and it is clear that this is a large community of warriors. The gathering is a circle around a campfire. Introductions are formal and scripted. We're not going to do much more than meet the famous warlord Nvwendee.

He's just come off his boat and smells strongly of whiskey and fish. He's a short man, hard as nails, but friendly. He greets us, tells some jokes, and everybody laughs. I have no idea what he is saying, but I smile big. If he has said anything that should offend me, Mulongo is not going to tell me.

Nvwendee is more than happy to pose for pictures, and we take several group shots. The meeting is pretty much over after that. Like so many pastoral calls, it's not what is said or done; it's simply that we were with them.

We make it back down to our boat in the dark, and in the dark, Éléphant navigates back upriver to the village with the Snake House, where we had stopped on our way to Kabalo. We'll spend the night there. The Chief of the Groupement, the group of villages in the area, wants to meet with us again tomorrow.

On its surface, this pastoral call we paid on Nvwendee's village in 2011 might seem insignificant. Why did we go to all that effort to stop and spend so much time waiting just for a photo opportunity? But that visit, Joseph's other pastoral calls, and his interaction with Nvwendee's daughter at the nursing school created connections between us and the village.

NVWENDEE'S VILLAGE

In July 2013, Taylor and I brought a small group of American women, including my wife Teri, to Mulongo. We had an opportunity for a more in-depth interview with Chatty. When she had heard that we were in Mulongo and that Joseph Mulongo needed some help hosting us, she walked two days to offer her help. When we met her this time, she looked different. She didn't look like a warrior in a simple, floor-length cotton dress. She certainly didn't look menacing, and I missed her poised, confident look. She looked like a poor woman in a secondhand dress that fit neither her body nor her personality.

She told her story to my wife Teri, daughter Taylor, and the other American women traveling with us. Mulongo translated; I listened. Chatty had been a school teacher before the war. When the war started, invading armies from Rwanda and Uganda came through the villages of her region, raping the women and burning their homes. The Congolese government soldiers were not able to defend these villages, and when they should have been liberating the villages, they were instead also raping and burning. Chatty joined the movement to defend the women of the villages. She called it a movement and called herself a Freedom Fighter.

Mulongo asked her bluntly, "Did you do any of these things we've heard?"

"No," she said. "I did not. I know that these things were done, but we did not do them." She continued, "Down south of here, there is violence. Here there is quiet."

I was thinking of the conversation I'd had with the pilot who'd brought us up to Mulongo. (I almost never fly in small planes, but I like to ride upfront with the pilot when I do. It's been a long time since I retired from the Marine Corps, but I'm pretty sure that if the pilot dropped dead from a heart attack, I could land the plane.) Thinking that I was new to the territory, he told me that even with all the Mai-Mai attacks on civilians, there had been no such attacks in the Mulongo District. He said that no one seemed to know why there was no violence in Mulongo. I chuckled; I knew why. When the other warlords started fighting again, Nvwendee and Chatty decided not to. (Everyone knows that Chatty is the brains behind Nvwendee.)

When the violence began again, Joseph Mulongo called Chatty on the cell phone. He asked, "Why are you Mai-Mai attacking villages again?"

"We're not," responded Chatty. "We are for peace, and we are not joining this movement toward violence."

When we had dinner with Bishop Ntambo later on that 2013 trip, Teri innocently mentioned that we had met Chatty. The Bishop was horrified. "You know that she is a cannibal! She chops up men with a machete and eats them! Of all the warlords, she's the worst."

There you have it: a woman with the reputation of a ruthless killer, feared by men, but who presents herself as a freedom fighter and defender of women. Did she lie to us? Was she guilty of the atrocities of this war? Here's how I figure it: I've become used to not knowing. On an emotional level, I'm so angry about the rape culture that continues to exist here that if a woman should take up a machete and chop off a raping soldier's manhood, I'm not that troubled.

I figure that the truth is somewhere in the middle. On the one hand, I can't believe that Chatty could have participated in this war and stayed above the violence. On the other hand, I figure that her reputation has grown beyond whatever she may have done to reach its current legendary status.

The present reality is that she is now becoming a leader for peace regardless of her past. She has found a place for her leadership skills to serve her village by enrolling in the nursing school in Mulongo. The transformation is not complete, but I can see her future. If she once was a mighty warrior wielding an AK47 or an avenging angel with a machete, she is now a community leader in a community on its way to peace.

Return by Land Cruiser

AFTER A NIGHT at the Snake House, we continue our 2011 river journey back to Mulongo, and I take up residence again in Dr. Serge's spare room.

The Cannondale T1 touring bike stood against my bedroom wall in Dr. Serge's house. Éléphant had washed it down and oiled all working parts. It was ready for the next leg of the ride. I picked it up by the saddle and handlebars and gave it a bounce. No loose parts. Then, I pushed down with all my weight.

Creak.

It made a creak.

I did it again.

Creak.

And again.

Creak, creak.

Maybe it's the saddle. Doesn't have to be something critical.

I looked over the frame. Every weld point.

There it was: a crack.

But maybe it's just the paint. It could be just that the paint has cracked.

But maybe the frame is cracked. All of the maintenance bulletins put out by Cannondale warn the owner not to ride on a cracked frame. Am I being a wimp or appropriately cautious?

It shouldn't be cracked. I know we've pounded it hard on the downhills, but not so hard as to crack the frame. This shouldn't be. If it is cracked, it is a manufacturing flaw, not abuse. The few times I've gone down on the bike, the crash has not been enough to damage my body, let alone the bicycle's frame.

What to do?

If we get out on the road with a cracked frame and it breaks, we're in a fix. This wouldn't be a problem if we had no time limits; we could set out and take whatever happened. If it broke, we'd find a local welder. He might even have skills in welding aluminum. After all, Land Rover bodies are aluminum.

At the beginning of the tour, this would not be such a big deal, but now, we are approaching a hard date on the calendar. If I'm late getting to Lubumbashi, I'll miss my flight. These are nonrefundable tickets; Teri would never forgive me if I messed up Spring Break in Ft. Myers.

I hesitate to speak up. This is a shame-motivated society, and I am a shame-motivated person. Confessing that my superior, American-built superbike has a crack in the frame is shaming. I'm going to have to tell Mulongo that we have a problem.

But there's another truth here that influences and confuses my thinking—I'm exhausted. I can't get my head excited about going up over the mountain, and I confess that to myself. This cracked frame is conveniently timed to rescue me from the final leg of this trip. But I'm not sure how I feel about that. On our 2010 ride, a washed-out bridge gave us the gift of a train ride to finish the journey. This year, I thought I wanted to make it back under my own power, but I realize now that I run out of steam physically and mentally at the end of these adventures. Physically, that means that my energy levels are getting depleted; I'm using more energy than I'm taking in. But this is also mentally exhausting for me, and two months seems to be my limit.

I share the news with Mulongo and share that I'm exhausted. He immediately agrees that the bicycle is unsafe and that he is not looking forward to riding over the mountain again. His agreement is so quick as to make me think that he is as relieved as I am that we should find another way. He's done for this trip.

Mulongo hears that Dr. Ivan is coming to town and goes to see if we can borrow his Land Cruiser. The other option is the Health Zone's ambulance, but our inconvenience is hardly a good use of an ambulance. Still, the ambulance may have an official reason to go south and could take us along.

Visit of Dr. Ivan, the Congressman

DR. IVAN'S ARRIVAL IN TOWN is a huge deal. He works and lives in Kinshasa now, and his trips back to Mulongo are few and far between. The village is getting stoked in anticipation of his arrival.

I'm learning that our preoccupation with developing circles of dependency is donor-centric thinking. There is, of course, a lot wrong with the socio-economic system here, but to read it as dependency on missionaries or foreign aid is missing what happens in real life when missionaries are not here or how outside assistance is used. I'm not saying that the way outside help is used is healthy; it's not. But what I'm beginning to see is that, while the aid is poorly used and results in a dysfunctional relationship with the outside world, this situation doesn't keep communities, on their good days, from seeing themselves as self-sufficient and being proud of it. This revelation is not one of understanding but of something else I don't understand well enough. This kind of revelation is getting to be common.

By refusing to be a player in development and by sitting here long enough, I've become invisible. I go off with the crowd to greet Dr. Ivan at the entrance to the village, the same place I was welcomed when I first arrived.

I'm not entirely without rank and am given a chair among the village dignitaries. It's an unbroken plastic chair—as much a comment on the village's opinion of a mzungu's inability to stand in the hot sun for hours, as it is a sign of respect. There must be a secret book somewhere on the care of a white person, filled with misinformation and thinly veiled contempt. Much the same as old reports read at the London Geographic Society that depicted indigenous Africans with tails.

But today is Dr. Ivan's day. I'm not invited, except that as long as I'm here, I'll be given a good chair to sit in. Not much else, though. As the reception takes shape, I'll be asked to relocate several times, always to a lower level of importance. The chief has turned out in a complete leopard-skin kit. For a short time, I'm seated next to him. We have a pleasant exchange in my limited French and his even more limited English. He's in a great mood and excited about Ivan's coming. Here is the intersection of traditional leadership with the young man the village sent off to parliament to represent them.

It doesn't take long before others come who need to be seated next to the chief, and I move down the line until I'm completely out of the dignitary group. I do get to keep my chair, though. However, position is more important than comfort: more important people are sitting on wooden stools, but they are closer to the action. I try a couple of times to give my chair to those of higher rank, but my courtesy is declined. I settle in, accepting my place as the invisible mzungu in the comfortable chair. It's going to be hours before Dr. Ivan's car appears, so there is plenty of time to watch the crowd.

The crowd changes shape several times as it grows. The official welcome becomes a communications center with a table full of mismatched amplifiers and speakers. A local radio DJ keeps the crowd engaged with music and updates on Dr. Ivan's estimated arrival time.

Flags of the various political parties are hung from the tree or displayed on tall poles. Ivan's party flag, brown with an elephant logo, dominates. My favorite flag is the old blue and gold flag of Kabila, the father. It spent a few years as the national flag and is now demoted to a political party's flag.

The adults are on my side of the road, and the children are on the other side. They push one another around to gain an advantage to see the parade. Scouts come out with switches to chase them back. The children run from the switches, squealing, but there isn't any fear. They come back around to regain their front-row positions.

The crowd of children again creeps out over the road as they leapfrog one another for the front. Attempts are again made to move them back, and a string is brought out to define the limit of where children can sit. That works for about three minutes. Finally, the children lose their patience with the wait and go off to play games. The clever ones climb trees to get a view, like Zacchaeus.

The big man finally arrives at the bridge that serves as the gateway into the village. Dr. Ivan is in a Land Cruiser Prada, the luxury 4X4 choice of those who can afford a car but need something that will handle these roads.

The crush of the crowd makes the planned reception impossible. There will be no receiving line of dignitaries. A man of the people, Dr. Ivan,

Visit of Dr. Ivan, the Congressman

gets out of the car and speaks to the crowd. Man, is he ever good at this! The people love him and hang onto his every word.

My first impression is that he's a lot younger than I imagined. I'm reminded of how young this country is compared to mine.

Ivan manages a few key handshakes and moves by foot toward the town center. The parade of people follows him. I make my way back to Serge's house, more invisible than before.

Later that afternoon, Ivan shows up at Serge's house. Ivan and Serge are close; Serge replaced Ivan as the hospital chief when Ivan went off to Kinshasa to represent the region in Congress, the lower house in parliament. Ivan is accompanied by his brother, Patrice, an attorney. Serge, Ivan, and Patrice sit in the living room talking. I can only try to follow in my weak French. I'm embarrassed at my lack of language skills. I'm not only embarrassed; this is the time when it all changes. I resolve to learn to speak French well enough to hold my own in this group.

In a corrupt political world, Ivan is a breath of fresh air.

Let me stop for a moment before you get ahead of me with your pre-loaded picture of the corrupt African politician. This place is corrupt, to be sure. Even the good guys have to play the game; it's the only game in town. However, the corruption here is created by a much larger corrupt system that has its origins in colonial-era expediency and is sustained by multinational, globalized, and legalized theft of the Congo's resources. It has an ugly history, and it has a present reality. I don't mind pointing out the corruption in Kinshasa as long as we are willing to track the money back to those in Europe, America, and China who are winning big in this corrupt game.

Back to Ivan. An honorable, honest man (or woman) doesn't stand a chance. Patronage systems run on honor, and both patrons and clients are invested in preserving it. The threat of losing honor by not providing carries more weight than the threat of being caught being dishonest. People will choose honor over honesty. Americans don't seem to understand this difference between honor and honesty. Around here, the difference is enormous.

It's not that Ivan is the only good politician I have met. I meet lots of them. In fact, I meet more good leaders than bad ones. Everywhere we go, I meet government administrators and traditional chiefs who want to do the right thing for the people they serve and lead. They can't beat the system, and the concentration of wealth in the hands of so few means that they never have the funds to provide the most basic services to their communities. They have to beg for schools, clinics, bridges, road repair, sanitation, wells, everything. The signs tell the story: every community development project has a sign naming the people who gave the money to finance the project: USAID built the clinic, the European Union gave the well, the Danish government cleared the landmines, UNICEF provided the school, the governor gave the bus, and his wife gave the orphanage. However, local leaders know the truth, and they don't hesitate to tell me: their taxes are stolen and taken to Kinshasa. Those responsible for essential community services are reduced to begging. I haven't yet decided if I want to call aid agencies and NGOs co-conspirators or dupes.

According to Ivan, Katanga Province produces enough in mineral-related taxes to fund its own development. By law, the fifty million dollars of taxes generated in Katanga from mining are to be returned to Katanga for community development. That's $12,000 a year for every village in Katanga, an annual amount that would change the world for those villages—far beyond what all the charity from the West can do.

Ivan challenged the government in Kinshasa with an open letter to the president asking for an accounting of the $50 million, as none of it got to the villages in Katanga. It didn't even get out of Kinshasa. When he ran for his seat the next election cycle, the election was blatantly stolen from him. So blatant was the election fraud that when he challenged the fraud in court, the seat was restored to him.

Today's talk has drifted into the recent news of the deaths in the village caused by rogue elephants running out of the forest.

I'm a conservationist, and I lament the loss of wildlife in this region. But sitting in the villages bordering the national forest, I have sympathy for those who cry out that the West cares more for the gorillas and elephants than they do for people. We hear stories of elephants driven out of the forest by rebels and militia who have poached everything with meat on its bones. The elephants run from the poachers into the villages, and they trample everything in their way, including men, women, and children.

Ivan says that he didn't go to Kinshasa to represent the elephants. "We're passing laws protecting the elephants, but we don't care if the people are suffering."

A List

brother and driver, Mulongo and I in Land Cruiser, Prada Luambo by nightfall.

stopping for gas

back home, decompression

Home in Indiana quiet time

Decompression

visit a few churches.

some success, but still can't articulate

Fondo

Editor's note: This page is Bob's list to himself, the things he was going to come back to later as we worked through this manuscript together. I've looked through his journals and notebooks and not found obvious drafts for the items in this list, so Taylor and I have chosen to leave this list as he wrote it—a record of incomplete thoughts. —Kate

Fondo d'Congo
Plainfield, October 2011

Editor's note: This chapter was originally a post on the Friendly Planet Missiology blog. It has been lightly edited to fit here. —Kate

A FONDO IS A NON-COMPETITIVE community bicycle ride. The word is Italian. So, add one more to the languages we have the joy of learning—Italian. The idea of a fondo is to gather hundreds of bicycle riders in a huge festival.

Mike Gilbert and his team of community developers did just that with the Fondo d'Congo. Making full use of the incredible Plainfield, Indiana park system, greenways, and county roads, they put together rides of varying lengths: 50 miles for the serious cyclist, 25 miles for those who thought 50 sounded a bit obsessive, and 10, 5, and 2-mile rides in and around the parks. Bikers in racing kit, families dressed for fun, hot dogs, BBQ, popcorn, balloons, frisbees, fire trucks, and firefighters. Fast road bikes, park cruisers, hybrids, mountain bikes, tandems, recumbents, children in buggies, dogs in baskets.

Guilford Township's Hummel Park, the largest township park in the state of Indiana, provided the big, new, beautiful Charleston Pavilion for the day. Gear Up Cyclery came to help with pre-ride maintenance issues. (Some of our riders were getting their bikes out of the garage for the first time in years.) A whole list of local businesses signed on as sponsors.

This Fondo was one day in Plainfield United Methodist Church's 175th-anniversary commitment to 175 straight days of risk-taking service and mission. With no central plan and only a large calendar in the narthex for coordination, members have created, and are delivering, a different service or mission project for each of the 175 days. Mike Gilbert decided that his contribution to the project would be to organize a fundraiser for Friendly Planet Missiology. He did that and so much more. The team delivering this event was huge, enthusiastic, and super competent. (Mike will be the first to modestly object to receiving this much credit.) In addition, as the Friendly Planet team keeps discovering, God has already prepared our success.

Yes, it was a fundraiser, and yes, many bicycles will be purchased for church and community leaders in the Democratic Republic of the Congo, but as our Congolese partners will testify, the biggest contribution an event like the Fondo d'Congo makes is the building of a connected global community. Friendly Planet Missiology now has an annual ride in Congo and an annual ride in Indiana. Maybe next year, we can have a Congolese rider at the Fondo, and maybe there is a Hoosier rider who would like to ride with us in the Congo.

The Fondo d'Congo will happen again, same time next year. For members of the bicycle community of central Indiana, it can be the warm-up ride for the Hilly Hundred. (Our 50-mile route has some vertical challenges.) It can be the last ride of the summer or the first ride of the fall. For families and friends, it is an opportunity for wholesome fun in the park. For those who think a lot about the suffering of people in faraway places, it is a way to connect and participate in their struggles.

On the River

The Third Tour

Going the Other Way

*or, An Introduction to the Third Tour
on the Congo River, January 2012*

The Friendly Planet Team's third tour in 2012 turns our route around in the other direction. We will be riding from Tenke up to Lubudi and then on to Kamina, where the bishop wants me to come to see him. I'm happy to do this because I want to retrace my 1998 ride through the Lubudi District, and I especially want to see Kansenia.

The team includes many of the same people, with some notable changes. Joseph Mulongo was elected the chief of the delegation to the 2012 General Conference of The United Methodist Church, held in Tampa. He is busier than can be, traveling to Lusaka, then to Liberia. So, Mumba will be taking his place as team leader. Two distinct teams have formed: the boat team wears the original teal blue FPM shirts; the bicycle team wears the bright yellow shirts of the Fondo d'Congo. We have no trouble recruiting team members.

With Mumba as team leader, the bicycle team will ride up to Kamina to see the bishop. Mumba has selected this team from the Tenke District and appointed a young pastor named Junior as his number two. Meanwhile, with Éléphant as captain and a local crew, Mary is going to run the boat team. The bicycle team will ride up to Kamina to see the bishop; the boat team will come down the Congo River to Bukama and pick the cyclists up there. Together, we'll take the *Indiana* to Mulongo.

We have new bicycles this year. We've purchased five mountain bikes from Zambikes in Lusaka. They are Trek bicycles, made in the Giant Bicycle factory in China, purposed for Africa and branded Zambike. We're going to give them a try. There's a risk here as we have no ready supply of spares.

After breakfast and team photos, we're off. I have no idea what day it is, and it's not my job to keep track.

Mumba leads the bicycle team north on a quite rideable dirt road. After 28 kilometers, we reach Tshilongo, a high point on the road that boasts three cell towers. It is also on the railroad track, so it has electricity. We stop just long enough to send quick greetings, and we're off again.

This countryside is spooky familiar. I can't pick out a particular landmark and say for sure, but I know I've been here before. Of course, I have. Back in 1998, I rode this route from Tenke up to Kansenia Gar. Here's a dilapidated train depot where we stopped for a meal, I think. Maybe it was a dream. Most of my time in the Congo in 1998 now feels like a dream. I was out here with men I didn't really know, in an inhospitable land, with no safe water to drink. (This was before bottled water.) There were rumors of a war breaking out just north of us. That didn't bother me, really. It was more that I was just lost: with no one to talk with, I was alone in my head. I can't say that I was afraid, just sort of lost, disoriented.

That ride was somewhere buried deep in my brain. I've lost so many memories from those years, but that ride is so central to who I have become that I recognize minor landmarks along the road—railroad crossings, bends in the road, even groves of trees. There's the depot where we stopped to find a place for the night, still the same ruined brick building, floor blackened by decades of charcoal fires.

That night, back in 1998, I was taken to an old Belgian farmhouse. I had no idea where we were going and no idea what we would find. It was the first night out on a journey of unknown length, a journey that was entirely outside my control. I was totally dependent upon my Congolese colleagues. We had met the day before, and we did not share a common language. This first night I will never forget.

The room I was taken to was large, high ceilinged, but clearly not lived in for years. There was an old mattress in one corner, and it reminded me of the sleeping spaces homeless people in the US set up for themselves wherever they can. My colleagues gave me a candle and a box of matches and left me on my own.

I was letting go of the need for control. All worries were melting away. No mosquito net, but no worry. Dark and alone, no worry. I had foolishly launched into an adventure with no plan, no worry. The room had the aura of a nightmare, but I was not dreaming yet. Somewhere between not dreaming and dreaming, I fell asleep and did not wake up until the sun came up. I woke up more on account of the heat than the light.

There was hot water for tea and some day-old bread for breakfast the next morning. We got an early start on the road to Kansenia, 50 or so kilometers away.

Kansenia Gar, Remembered

Kansenia Gar in 1998 is when the world changed for me.

It was the first of my bicycle adventures, and I was riding my Cannondale F500 mountain bike. We hit Kansenia Gar on the third day.

Kansenia has three distinct forms. Kansenia Gar is the railroad station on the tracks that run along the ridge. In the valley, there's Kansenia Mission, the old Catholic mission station and girls' school, and Kansenia Village, where the people live.

The seven-kilometer ride from Kansenia Gar to Kansenia Mission took us along the ridge and down into the valley. It is the most beautiful valley I've ever seen. It stretches to the horizon and is encased in a horseshoe-shaped mountain ring. It is a shade of green I had never seen before like a new color was just invented for this valley. I felt like we were standing over Shangra-La, or like we had been transported to some vegetation-rich planet previously undiscovered.

We had to follow the steep, zig-zagging, washed-out gravel road to get down into the valley. As soon as we began the descent, a small group of young men arrived to help us down. Happy for the help, I handed my loaded mountain bike over to one of them. Not wanting the visual of a white missionary followed by a line of porters, I walked along behind.

On the way down, we walked through a small river of waterfalls.

At the bottom, we walked past the mission. Its classic colonial architecture was out of place in the jungle. In the colonial period, many important Congolese families sent their daughters to this prestigious boarding school for a quality education. Even then, this was unusual and represented the antithesis of the Belgian attitude toward educating the Congolese, which is to say, not educating them. In 1998 it seemed strange that people here remembered a time when girls, at least those from the elite families, went to good schools. It doesn't appear that the school is still functioning as a boarding school, and if it is still open, it's barely alive.

I thought that if I needed a place to spend the night, we might stay at the mission, but we passed on by. At this point, people from the village had joined our walk, and we were headed for the United Methodist church.

The United Methodist Church in Kansenia Village was not much of a building. Certainly, compared to the mission, it was a hut. That's just the point. The Catholic mission was colonial in its construction. The United Methodist church had been built by its congregants with their own resources. It had low walls of locally baked bricks with a sagging grass roof hanging over the walls all the way to the ground. We were invited inside and ducked through the door into the dark sanctuary. The floor was dirt. The roof was supported by unmilled tree trunks three down the center aisle. The room was packed with excited worshippers. I was taken to the front and given a bamboo tripod chair so that we could have church.

Worship services in these village churches have been some of my favorite times. The theology is Christian, and the acts of worship are locally rooted. The Congolese Methodists have brought their traditional drums, singing, and dancing into the church. It is raw, and it is beautiful.

After worship, a woman brought her sick child and two chickens to us in the pastor's hut. I was asked to pray for the child. Sure, Christian pastors all over the world enter homes and pray for the sick. But this was way more like the role of the traditional healer. There was an expectation of appeasing God with the offering of the chickens.

It was at Kansenia Gar in 1998 that I began to listen. This was the deep listening that eventually became my Doctor of Ministry thesis, *Scripture as a Tool of Community Development*. There's a copy of it in the library at Christian Theological Seminary in Indianapolis, and I have the only other copy. I was so unhappy with the writing, that I only ordered one souvenir copy for myself to disappear on my bookshelf, and I didn't file it on the seminary's electronic search engine for others to find it. Perhaps someday, I'll rewrite it into a readable book and publish it.

After we had climbed back out of the valley, we were offered beds for the night in the home of the train station manager, a United Methodist lay leader. As was the pattern, I got the good bed—old, sagging springs, worn cover, small dark room, but comfortable and clean.

Our host suggested that he could get us on the train to Lubudi, our next destination. That would save us a whole day of riding. He did not tell us the train was a freight train, and I didn't think to ask. I was learning to leave the planning to my Congolese colleagues.

In the morning, we went to the station to wait. As the district superintendent and I sat on the stoop, we watched a local farmer lead a team of traction cows pulling a cart into the station yard. The cart was carrying bags of maize that would be loaded onto the train bound for Lubudi. We, the United Methodists in the Lubudi district, had nothing like this team of cows. The church's cornfields were sources of needed income and food for district conference gatherings. While we were touring the churches, we inspected the cornfields and saw that our farmers were tilling these fields by hand.

I asked the district superintendent how much a team like that would cost, and he figured that with cart and plow, the team would cost under $2,000. This was where I first began to question the mission model we were using. The United Methodist Church, through the General Board of Global Ministries, had two agricultural mission stations in Katanga. One was run by a salt of the earth evangelical couple from Ohio who, out of compassion for the Congolese people, had moved a whole farm from Ohio to Zaire in shipping containers, the shipping containers then being repurposed as barns. The wife was a nurse, and she established a clinic. With the clinic's establishment, the village around the mission swelled from 10,000 to 40,000 instantly. But, because they used technologies not available to local farmers, there was no expectation that the mission would continue beyond the missionaries' stay. And it didn't.

There's so much positive that I could say about these missionaries—their faith, courage, compassion, humility, humor, hard work, sacrifice, and love—but I cannot affirm the model. And the thing is, the model was not really their choice—it was a community choice. That model had been chosen by the church that sends missionaries and the communities that receive them. In any event, the project didn't survive their departure with all the other missionaries in 1998.

A former Peace Corps couple ran the other agricultural mission station. It was located in the district's other episcopal area and on the other end of the theological spectrum. The hallmarks of that station were appropriate technology and crop experimentation, grounded in local knowledge and resources. Even so, for whatever reason, they never developed a healthy working relationship with the church.

Both missionary couples would argue vigorously with me on these points, and I'm sure they are reading this now and arguing with the book. But from the stoop at Kansenia Gar, where I sat with the Lubudi district superintendent in 1998, that's what I saw.

Just a couple of weeks before, I had been listening to the ham radio missionary channel and heard that the missionaries were looking for seed corn. At the same time, on the separate church channel, the Lubudi district superintendent was trying to sell seed corn. I marveled at the disconnect. There was a missionary world and a church world, but they were not integrating. The missionaries thought they mixed, but a clear divide, a wall, separated them. The missionary community's lack of awareness of the separation was probably the piece that made me the angriest.

When I moved to Likasi, the Baptist missionary family had just moved back to the States, which meant I was the only white missionary in Likasi. This city used to boast several missionary families, and there used to be enough white families in Likasi to support the local private swimming pool. Then I was it, the pool was closed, and people asked the unbelievable question: "What's it like to be the only one in Likasi?" Of course, the complete question was, "What's it like to be the only *white person* in Likasi?" That bothered me. That, and the passed down missionary handbook that, on the first page, taught me how to reprimand my houseboy in Swahili for bringing me tea that was too cold. Maybe there might have been a day when I might have wanted to say that my tea was too cold, but should that have been on the first page of the manual?

So, the real question was: do the Congolese church leaders want two missionary-run agricultural mission stations, or would they prefer a team of traction animals? The answer was complex in 1998 and still is today. They would, of course, prefer to have the team of cows, or better, a tractor, but they know too well that the money doesn't come without a missionary. Does the community want a missionary? Of course.

The train's arrival interrupted my reflections. It was a big surprise, to me, at least. Maybe everyone else knew that it would be a freight train.

Our bicycles were loaded in a boxcar, and the district lay leader stayed with them. The rest of us were put inside a brand-new Volvo bus painted in the colors and design of the new DRC flag, all white and blue and gold. The bus was riding on a flat car facing backward.

Riding with us on the bus were a half dozen armed soldiers. I'm not sure if they were guarding the bus or had hitched a ride, as we had.

Greetings were cordial but brief. There wasn't going to be a lot of chatting. And there wasn't going to be any photography. Although we were in a time of peace, between the fall of Mobutu and the coming war, there was still tension riding in a bus on a train with armed soldiers.

The ride to Lubudi took 4 hours. The bus was facing backward and rocked on the flat car as the train rocked on the tracks, but not in sync. This trip was an important lesson in leadership for me. I was learning to listen and not question my Congolese colleagues' decisions. I was learning to trust the ideas in my head and practice the things I had written about in my thesis.

Kansenia to Lubudi, 2012

THE ROAD FROM KANSENIA to Lubudi is a private farm road. When the Friendly Planet bicycle team arrives at the guardhouse protecting the road in 2012, we discover that the permission we believe we have has not been relayed to the guards. Several phone calls are made to the farm manager in Lubumbashi to get it all straightened out. I just get comfortable waiting a safe distance from the debate, which gets heated at times.

Eventually, the issues are resolved, some cash changes hands, and we ride on.

The landscape through here is a high plateau. It's flat, with tall grass and far-off tree lines. We can see that we are level with the mountains in the distance. The riding is easy. Not only is the road flat, but it hasn't been destroyed by the heavy trucks.

One of the treats of this adventure is the middle of nowhere surprises. We ride through the ruins of Biano. My colleagues barely notice, and they say nothing. It's not an African village. It looks like an old hotel, maybe, or a once-grand estate. I can imagine the former beauty of the house's colonial architecture. People live here like in a dystopian story: some catastrophic event ended its glory days, and now squatters occupy the ruins. A bit further up the road, we pass a square shell of a building near the railroad with the sign "Biano" fading on the façade. Post office? Customs house?

When we reach Lubudi, I'm still thinking about the colonial days and the impossibility of restoring those old buildings. Then wonder whether my misguided thought might even be a good idea. We ride in the back way through the forest, and this road takes us by the old cement factory.

A house that used to be the home of one of the Belgian factory executives is for sale. My colleagues suggest I buy it for our office despite the horrible shape it's in and the quarter-million-dollar price tag. The prices of real estate here are unbelievable.

The building that intrigued me the most, though, was the executive club, the old bar for the white executives of the cement factory. It's a reminder of the days when there were large European populations here, even in remote towns like Lubudi. It's a reminder of two worlds existing in the same place on two separate planes.

After independence, Congolese businessmen moved into the places vacated by the departing Europeans. This practice highlights a problem here: the model of colonial society has remained, almost as if there were an expectation of those days returning. It's like putting on a power suit that you found at a thrift store. It doesn't fit right, and it doesn't look like you, but you wear it anyway because you think you need a suit, and this is the one you have.

We head for the convent of the Benedictine Sisters. On our previous trips to Lubudi, we've learned that they provide a clean and safe room.

The United Methodist Church has a long history here. Back in 1998, on my first visit by bicycle, Lubudi proved to be the exception to the dependent patronage begging we found in all the other villages. During that bicycle tour, our meetings typically began with worship and then shifted into a meeting with the church leadership, where a list of needs was presented to the missionary. I hated this part in every church we visited. Even then, I resisted the model of the missionary as a patron.

But the Lubudi church was different. Built in the late 1920s, the Lubudi United Methodist Church was a small brick chapel that had stood the years well. In 1998, it was the only United Methodist church in the Lubudi District that was of "permanent construction," but the congregation had outgrown its small chapel. Plans were being made for a new large sanctuary.

As I sat and heard the reports from the various church groups, I noticed a difference in tone from the reports I had become used to hearing. Though I did not speak the language, the similarity of the reports from church to church taught me to understand many of the words and follow the speaker's intonation.

The Lubudi reports had an optimism and a pride of ownership that the others had lacked. They were not depressing with begging but rather filled with bragging. The construction committee, led by two engineers from the cement factory, reported the number of loads of stones for the foundation that had been collected. These engineer leaders were from Kinshasa and Lubumbashi. They had university degrees, they had ideas and dreams, and they had the self-assurance necessary to pull them off.

Kansenia to Lubudi, 2012

The men's group had plans for a grain mill that would generate the cash income needed for the cement and roofing. Instead of asking me for the money to purchase the mill, they told me how much they had already raised and the plan to raise the rest. The women reported the creation of a foyer, a women's school, where they were teaching basic literacy and home skills. They were collecting "dues" from their members to buy a sewing machine.

Then the choir reported. The choir members gave me a list of all the things the choir needed: robes, music, and a keyboard. The room erupted at them, "That's not how we do it now!" It was all I could do to keep the peace. In my heart, I was thrilled at the verbal beatdown the choir was getting from the rest of the leadership, but I didn't want to see them destroyed.

I kept the report on the table, hoping that some solutions to the stated needs would emerge over the course of the meeting. There was no way I was going to buy them a keyboard. I'm a drums person. If the choir wanted to go modern, they'd have to fund it themselves. I was clueless about what they meant by needing music, so I didn't go there. The robes were another story. In truth, I had a box full of hand-me-down choir robes in the depot in Likasi. Choirs all over America were cleaning out their closets and shipping their old robes to Africa. What's wrong with that?

What's wrong is that the Congo was famous for its cotton and had a thriving textile industry at one time. By 1998, the local fashion sense had been devalued by both those good-hearted Americans who were flooding Africa with second-hand clothing and by the Congolese themselves who abandoned their own textile skills for discarded American choir robes. This state of affairs is wrong on so many levels, so instead of offering up the American cast-offs, I suggested the possibility of the choir and the women's school working together to create new robes with their new sewing machines.

On our current trip in 2012, I'm surprised to see that the church construction has stalled. When a small rural church in Indiana was rebuilding after a tornado, they decided to build a church in the Congo with a tithe of their building funds. They gave me $10,000, and I gave it to Bishop Ntambo to give to Lubudi. That amount should have been enough to leverage the rest of the community assets to finish the church. Instead, the new church in Lubudi is half-finished. Something happened in the leadership. I'm curious to find out, but I can't stay here. I can't become their missionary, and I can't own their problem, even though part of me wants to.

Lubudi is one of the places where I would enjoy living if I were to be a stationed missionary again. There is electricity thanks to a turbine generator in a waterfall five kilometers north of town. You can get right up close to the waterfall and feel its power. The turbine is huge and loud, from the days when electricity was generated by dynamos the size of locomotives, with a steampunk feel. It's like walking into a world that is giant scale. I feel like Jack after he climbed the Beanstalk, or like Gulliver in Brobdingnag, the land of giants. The scale is off.

The cement factory is equally ancient and a monster from the age of machines, and I'm told it is so worn out that it operates at just ten percent of its capacity. It's the poster child of the habit of working old, colonial-era factories into the ground. If there is one lesson that has not been learned here, regardless of how many times it's been demonstrated, it is the need to reinvest in business, industry, and community.

On a personal note, I notice an old Land Rover sitting on blocks in the garage of the cement factory. If I lived here, I'd find out who owns it, negotiate for it, and then find a good mechanic to restore it.

It is amazing. This country is wasting away toward absolute poverty amid the most remarkable diversity of natural resources. The Congo River drops a mile from its source around Kolwesi, with hundreds of tributaries featuring tremendous waterfalls. Electricity should be free for every household. In the middle of a worldwide cement shortage, Katanga is importing cement when there is all the limestone and gypsum you need right here in the mountain back yard of Lubudi. Katanga should be exporting cement. This region should be not only a breadbasket for the Congo but a food exporting region. No one should be hungry here. Cotton and the textile industry should be famous again. And this list doesn't even mention the minerals in the ground. Why? Why do the people starve in the midst of all of these resources? What's the problem? Who are the bad guys? Is there a fix? Can the Church do anything? Is the Church part of the problem? I have so many questions.

This time we stay a couple of days in Lubudi. We had passed through during the night on our first tour and didn't even come this way on the second. We have to sit a spell and enjoy the hospitality.

Zambikes

WE DISCOVER A THING or two about the new Zambikes along the way to Lubudi. First, as the roads are made of sharp rocks, the tires on the Zambikes get cut badly. And now that the bikes have put on some kilometers and have been pounded on the rocks, we have a few other issues.

Second, when we go looking for a bicycle shop, we find one. The bike shop is mostly outdoors, a classic shade tree mechanic. He has a welder in a shed, where he rebuilds frames. There are just a few simple tools in his toolbox, nothing that looks like a bike shop tool, but he can fix our bikes. No problem. This mechanic has no fear of the fancy-schmancy, multi-speed, modern mountain bike.

Bikes fixed, gear packed, we say our goodbyes in the early morning, and we're off again. Good to be back on the bike.

We're carrying a live turkey on one of the Zambikes. We were given two turkeys, one from the chief and one from the church in Lubudi. One of them we left with the district superintendent, and one we took with us.

Lubudi to Luena

AT MIDDAY, WE COME to Buyofwe. On our first bicycle tour two years ago, the bridge had been out, and we had to finish the journey by train from Luena to Tenke. The old bridge has been replaced by a new steel girder bridge. The river below is a long way down and is running pretty fast, but I'm thinking that we might have been able to make the crossing by pirogues if we had pushed the issue on our previous ride. At the time, though, we gave that decision to the local church leadership. It was their call.

This new bridge is one lane wide and about 300 yards long. It took two years to build and has just opened. However, the road up to and down from the bridge has yet to be repaired. As it now stands, it would still be difficult for a truck to get up on the bridge or down from it, but it is no problem for bicycles.

At the end of this day's long ride, Luena welcomes us. The church is organized for our arrival because their leadership is in tune with the program. They get us.

They've made the Pilot's House ready for us, and food is on its way. We have buckets of water for our bathing, and the beds are all made up for us. Electricity has been turned on in the house so we can recharge our phones, laptops, and my Nook, even though the cell connection is not quite strong enough to get online. Gaston is the UMC missionary pilot who delivers medicines, vital supplies, and guests to the villages around the North Katanga and Lubudi Districts. He also does medical evacuations when necessary. He's not in Luena often, but this is the house he uses when he's here.

We spend the next day touring the church's active projects, and although local leaders have taken over from the missionaries, none have broken out of the old model. Nowhere do I see anything new—nothing created since the missionaries left. I first saw these projects back in 1991. On the one hand, I marvel at how the local leadership has been able to keep these projects going with no resources coming from the outside. But on the other hand, they have not been able to leverage sufficient local resources to fund them beyond bare survival. They are stuck. They have inherited these missionary projects and take some pride in now owning them, but they can't yet imagine a new way to do them.

We go up to the top of the hill overlooking Luena. Here is where John Enright had brought us in '91 to see the new church he was building. It was to be a large, octagon-shaped sanctuary, a feat of engineering genius. And it was being constructed with locally salvaged materials. The beams were reclaimed railroad rails, bent by brute force around a big tree and welded on site. This is why I called John the "MacGyver of missionaries."

It was quite the dream. The view from this spot is inspiring, and when finished, the building would have been the crown of Luena. It was never finished. Only the outer walls remain, and all the beams and roofing sheets have been cannibalized for a more modest, rectangular church building on the site. This building, too, though, is unfinished.

I had determined not to make these tours about missionaries, and this book is not supposed to be about missionaries and their projects, but this is what I'm finding. The old missions have been picked up by local leadership, but they don't have the resources to finish them, and they don't have a new model for the work. Let me be clear, I don't know what that new model needs to look like, but I'm sure that the old one is no longer working.

It is a good visit to Luena. No stress. We get to see more of the church and community than before, and I feel like we are getting a more honest picture. Their hospitality is genuine and without agenda. And the discussions around the work are frank, neither hiding problems nor begging for help. Luena is another one of those places where I would enjoy working if I were stationed there. But there are too many of these places, and a stationed missionary cannot be the solution.

Luena to Bukama

BUKAMA, LIKE LUENA, IS HOT. Like Lubudi, it is rocky.

Bukama is a port on the Congo River, and it is from here that we can catch our boat to Mulongo. But first, we have to go up to Kamina.

The district superintendent of the Bukama District has arranged for our stay in a hotel down on the tracks near the docks. This is straight out of a Joseph Conrad novel. The hotel is below street level behind a row of shops. The street is busy with buying and selling everything you can imagine you need, from radios to razor blades, and all kinds of things plastic in bright colors. Someone has a local DJ on a loudspeaker.

The hotel itself is a row of rooms along a walled garden. Everything is painted white with green trim. Not too bad. Actually, kind of cool. My room is a single with no ceiling, so I'm looking at the holes in the roof. The toilets and baths are in a separate building, and I'm given the key to the toilet that will be mine exclusively while I'm here. The bath is just a block room with a gravel floor and a drain to the outside.

The walled garden includes a large outdoor eating area. The district women fill this space with a huge feed, and most of the evening is taken up in food preparation and eating.

As the night goes on, the loudspeaker blasts a locally recorded rock ballad with several movements and a couple of great riffs. It's good. I like it. It comes on a regular cycle through the night. This night has almost nothing to do with the mission we're on, but I'll remember it as the coolest of nights. This is adventure travel in the shipping yards along the Congo River, with a soundtrack.

The district superintendent has planned a day for us to visit a couple of villages in his district. We get our bicycles and ride up the tracks. Mostly, we walk our bikes, the tracks being not as rideable as hoped.

In one village, we sit down with the chief to talk about development. He talks. We listen. I don't get it all, but he's got an opinion about wells and the types of pumps being installed. He has a suggestion that would make these pumps better. I'm wondering who else is sitting and listening to this chief.

He gives us a goat. This is awkward. How do you transport a goat if you come on a bicycle? Sometimes, when we are given a goat, we assign a local boy scout to get it back to the superintendent's house. This time, the goat is small enough that the team straps him to the rear rack of one of the Zambikes.

We're off to See the Bishop
Bukama to Kamina

IT'S A TWO-DAY RIDE from Bukama to Kamina. We'll break at Kabando Dianda for a meal. The road forks there: east goes toward Nyembo Umpunga, north to Kamina.

We'll overnight in Kibula.

Kibula is in the catchment of the Kamina-based projects. Its location along the railroad makes it easy to get to, and being easy to get to makes it attractive to development projects. Here is one observation: development projects follow the easiest paths. My biggest complaint of big NGO development projects is that they barely penetrate the surface of the need. The outsiders think they have reached the end of the world when they are barely inside the country. Beautiful model projects are set up in accessible communities where staffers and volunteers can come in and build and where dignitaries can fly in and marvel.

We arrive early enough to spend some quality time with ourselves as a team. Our first order of business is to repair the tires, which have worn thin on the rocks. The only complaint I have of the Zambikes is the tires. I understand the need for the company to keep the cost of the bikes low, but their choice to go cheap on the tires has given us a problem. These tires are shot, and there are no spares anywhere in all of Katanga, so Junior is sewing up the ripped tires. My tires are fine only because I brought a fresh set from the States.

Our sleeping room is what is called the UMCOR House. UMCOR is the United Methodist Committee on Relief, and Methodists tend to be very proud of its work. Saying anything remotely negative about UMCOR to a United Methodist back in the States is the equivalent of insulting the American flag or Mom's apple pie. The UMCOR House in Kibula shows that even this NGO has feet of clay.

The UMCOR House is a two-room brick house with a metal roof of relatively recent construction. No one lives in it.

The UMCOR house is, in fact, a soymilk project. Inside is the machine that converts soy into milk. Pristine. Unused. Kept safe under lock and key. The door is padlocked. It's like it is being guarded so that no damage comes to it. I'm reminded of the Jesus parable where the one servant buried the talent given him, thinking that protecting it would please his master.

The UMCOR House is the nicest house in the village, and it makes sense to put the visitors here for the night.

The UMCOR House is the perfect example of what development projects look like when the people who built them go home. Somewhere, somebody decided that what the people of Kibula needed was a soymilk project to benefit children's health and establish a local business. Makes sense.

However, the village leadership asked me why UMCOR set up a soymilk project when what Kibula needed was a clinic. They showed us the grass-roofed paillotte that served as their clinic and told us there were no meds.

Sure, the soymilk project probably would make sense if there were some local energy around it. In the long run, it might make more sense even than the clinic. A clinic is a deep hole, never self-sufficient, an eternal dependency. A soymilk project could create profits as it lifted the general health of the community. It does make sense.

However, this project is here because it is close to the UMCOR base in Kamina. The people who brought it here thought they had reached out into a remote village, when in reality, they are barely outside of town.

This trip is turning negative for me.

I'm beginning not to like going to Kamina because it's NGO City. Everybody with a white truck and an acronym for a name is here, and there is an obscenity of aid. Like the American frontiersman, when the farmers start arriving, I feel the need to move on.

The bishop has called us to come to Kamina to meet with him. He wants us to see all the work in Kamina. Specifically, he wants me to witness all the successful projects he has going in Kamina. There are constant rumors in the States that African bishops misuse the funds sent to them.

He wants me to tell all the Americans how much is getting accomplished in Kamina. Bishop Ntambo thinks I am a credible witness, but the problem with his plan is that I don't sit at any of the tables within the UMC hierarchy where these things are discussed.

I've been intentional about keeping Friendly Planet's work separate from Bishop Ntambo's in order to build up a second base. But now seems to be a good time to see what he is doing and report what we are doing to him. So, we go to Kamina to see the bishop, and guess what? The bishop isn't there. He has sent word that he is delayed in Lubumbashi and will join us soon. We should wait.

I'm settled into the United Methodist Guest House. I have no idea where the other members of the bicycle team are staying, but everyone has a relative in Kamina, so it's not a worry. This guest house is one of my safe places in the Congo. I've been staying here since 1991, and it's become as comfortable to me as an old shoe. Back then, it was the home of missionaries Ken and Deb Vance, and Taco Tuesday with them is a fond memory. The house was trashed in the pillage of '91 as Ken, Deb, and other missionaries fled from here to the airstrip under gunfire. When Bishop Ntambo rebuilt the conference center in 1998, he had missionaries Tom and Liz Ryder move up from Lubumbashi to establish the treasurer's office in Kamina since Tom was the field treasurer for the General Board of Global Ministries. Tom and Liz went shopping in South Africa for all the fixtures and furnishings to fully restore and upgrade this shellshocked house. Not long after they succeeded at making it pleasant, they became part of the great evacuation as the new war forced us all out. Once again, the house was looted for all its furniture and plumbing.

Tom and Liz fell into that category of missionaries that I would call world adventurers. They enjoyed the life of expatriates in a foreign land. They loved to travel, didn't mind the chaos, and served wherever they were sent. They weren't particularly theological. Tom was an accountant, retired from civil service, giving the Church his time and talent in exchange for meaning and adventure. Liz was a nurse, and she always created some local project to make the world a better place. They get no points from me on their missiology, but the world would be better if there were more people like them. Of all the Americans in the Congo, they were the ones I would go to when I needed a fix of unconditional hospitality, some familiar food, a beer, and R-rated movies.

We're off to See the Bishop

Hey, I swore this was not going to be about missionaries, but I can't stay in the guest house in Kamina without the memories of missionaries. After the war in the late '90s, when Bishop Ntambo rebuilt the conference center for the second time, he rebuilt this house as a guest house. It has hosted several Congolese dignitaries, including the President, but mostly it is for visiting Americans.

I do some walking around Kamina solo. This time, I'm looking for the ruins of the colonial town. There's plenty of evidence if you know what you're looking for. I spot the old brewery, the railroad station, and the social club swimming pool.

The old brewery stands as a monument to colonial reach, a kind of marker of how far the colonial authorities made it into the interior. Only the Catholic convents are deeper into this land than the breweries. Congo is known for its quality beers, but this brewery is down to a skeleton crew and no output, just managers on the payroll keeping the place secure for whenever it restarts, if ever.

In this Methodist town, the Methodists—who are non-drinkers—tell me that the brewery shut down because of the conflict between the primarily Methodist and non-drinking Luba and the Kasai to the north, who were the brewery's customers. It would be wrong to call the wars in the DRC tribal, but when the wars break out, tribalism also comes out. There is undoubtedly more to the decline of this factory than the loss of customers through a tribal falling out, such as poor upper management and inconsistent transportation for moving bottles to market. But it strikes me as a bit of a shame that the United Methodists do not see breweries for their potential in community development. When you have a working brewery in town, you have good water. The same could be said for a Coca-Cola bottling plant. This brewery also bottled soft drinks. I get the concern over the evils of alcohol consumption, and I've seen it bad here, but maybe we could find a middle ground. Perhaps if they didn't put the beer in those huge bottles, that would be a start.

The pool is in ruins, but I can make out the footprint and the changing rooms. So much of what is Kamina, especially the Ville, was whites only, and it's hard to imagine enough white families lived here to fill all these spaces. Standing at the ruins of the pool, I think about race and the racism that hangs over this place. The whites are gone, but the poison is still here.

It wasn't like Blacks couldn't mix with whites. They could join the club. They simply had to pass a test to prove that they were civilized enough to socialize with white families. The test included a home visit where they had to eat like a European, using the correct fork and such. Those who passed were issued a card that said they were *evolved*. That's what the card was called, an *evolved* card. I'll leave you with that to stew on.

Another day, Mulongo and I walk together downtown to the United Methodist Conference Center. It's an impressive building in the business section, the first significant public building to be rebuilt after the war. Bishop Ntambo has not only rebuilt the United Methodist Church up from the ashes but has also led the whole community back. In 2012, Kamina is a bustling upcountry crossroads, a railhead with a key military base five kilometers outside of town. The streets are full of UN peacekeeping trucks and the trucks of every NGO in the alphabet soup of international development.

Over the street is a banner announcing the coming of the anti-malaria campaign and bed net distribution. Mulongo says to me, "Look at that banner. It makes me angry." I looked and saw what he was seeing. The title sponsors of the program are UMCOR and the Ministry of Health. Unless you happen to know that UMCOR is an agency of the United Methodist Church—and the person on the street has no way of knowing that—you only know that some NGO from the US or Europe is funding a Ministry of Health program. What boils my blood is that the country has more than enough wealth to fund a first-class Ministry of Health. So, this is a prime example of the accepted model for helping a rich country out of its poverty. The outside agency provides the money, and the inside agency provides the distribution and cashes in. The problem is that the inside agency would have all the money it needs if it were not for corruption and patronage practices. Some high-ranking Ministry of Health director will take his cut of the distribution, resell those nets on the black market, and make a killing.

Meanwhile, our people, Congolese United Methodists, will have to get nets by buying them in the market. One of our team purchased two treated nets for himself marked "CDC, Not for Resale" in a remote village market. Similarly, we often see motorcycles loaded with cornmeal bags marked "USAID" coming down from the war zone. Food distributed free in one zone is resold in another.

I'm wondering how mad the average pew-sitting United Methodist in the US might be if they knew that the Ministry of Health was getting credit for their generosity. How would they feel to know that the leadership infrastructure their mission giving had spent 100 years building up was being overlooked in this grand program? What makes Mulongo fume is that while this giant parachute drop program raises and spends millions of United Methodist dollars, the pastors and lay leaders of the local United Methodist churches starve and suffer from malaria for lack of support. And on top of that, they are not involved in the delivery of the program. In the United Methodist Church, we value the Connection—the interrelationships of all United Methodists. This means that we already have a delivery structure—the Connection—and it's being underutilized. It's all a mess.

The free distribution of mosquito nets in Kamina will be a good show, but it won't affect the communities outside of Kamina one bit. The top of the food chain will take them for themselves, and people back in the States will happily think that they've given to poor Africans. I've got to get out of this town. Everywhere I look, there's a reminder of how truly effed up our attempts at helping are.

A Meeting at the Guest House
Kamina

WITH THE BISHOP ABSENT, the district superintendents—both friends and all-around good guys—step in to give us tours of their districts. Kamina has enough United Methodist congregations that it has been split into two districts—Kamina-Ville and Kamina-Cité—following the dividing line left over from the colonial period.

There was a meeting to plan the district visits held in the living room of the guest house. The guest house makes an excellent place to have meetings, but the house is only open for these meetings if a guest is here. Once more, I learn the lesson of my purpose: I serve no function in these meetings other than being the justification for the meeting. The church in the Congo is fully capable in its leadership, delivery of ministry, or anything else it chooses to do. Someone like me is not required, except that it takes someone like me to create a reason to do something. Functionally, I'm as useless as a screen door on a submarine, but I do serve a purpose.

Over time, I will learn that the community uses me in two ways. First, I am a catalyst for activity, and my appearance breaks up the monotony of life that has a stranglehold on creativity and progress. Second, the community expects me to find the resources for their projects.

Kamina is a boomtown of development work, but the church sees nearly none of this outside money. The bishop has a handful of pet projects that started with agency grants or large donations. But these projects struggle after the initial enthusiasm has worn off and the reality of the depth of poverty has sunk in. However, this time, we will not be seeing what most visitors are shown when the bishop is in charge of the visit, but what the next level of leadership down struggles with. These are the leaders who follow in the footsteps of the bishop but don't receive any of the funding.

What I'm seeing is that not only is there a vast resource gap between Kamina and the remote districts like Mulongo and Kabalo, but there is also a resource gap within Kamina itself. The local churches are expected to fend for themselves based on the idea that a local congregation should be able to organize itself and fund itself with people's tithes. I get the argument, and I shared the belief early on, but I've come to disagree with myself on this point. I think we have it backward.

We will gladly fund a school, a clinic, or a feeding program, but not a church. An argument is beginning to take shape in my head: fund the church. Pay the pastor a living wage. Build solid sanctuaries. Include a parsonage. Then, set the church to the task of community development. Let the church build the clinics and the schools. Let the church dig the wells and whatever else the community needs.

Of course, this couldn't be a parachute drop program—that would not work any better than any of the other parachute drop programs have worked. Instead, this would require teaching, preaching, and training. The United Methodist Church has been in the DRC for 100 years now. While the missionary era has had its flaws, the net result has been an extensive and effective ministry delivery system. Just a few tweaks are all it needs to take this into the future.

When he was first elected bishop, Ntambo put forward a vision for the United Methodist Church in North Katanga, beginning with the pastor's life. He commissioned a local artist to draw the vision of a pastor's home and churchyard, complete with chickens and a fishpond. It was Gainsborough-esque in its idyllic representation.

Now, I think he was right. That's where you start. Feed the pastors, and they will feed the flock.

Bishop Ntambo has all but abandoned his vision. He pulls it out from time to time, but he can't get funding for it in practice. He gets funding for agricultural projects, which limp along. He gets funding for health initiatives that fail to reach the remote districts for lack of delivery infrastructure. He gets funding for an orphanage because, well, orphanages are trending. But he can't sell his vision for his pastors. He's right on this, and the rest of the world is wrong.

Church Tours in and around Kamina

WE RIDE OUR BICYCLES from the guest house in the *ville* over to the *cité* side of Kamina. Here the homes reflect local building practices, mostly mud-brick and thatch or fired brick and tin, instead of the ville's colonial architecture. The cité streets are more crowded with people, goats, and rubbish. Our visit begins at the district superintendent's home. Inside, I'm fascinated by the ceiling made of some kind of woven matting, decorative like a tin ceiling, only in bamboo. There's a nature video running on the TV—even Congolese city-dwellers must learn about wildlife from a television show. As lovely as this house is, I learn that it's a rental, a rental the district superintendent can't afford, and his family will be looking for a new place soon.

Next, we head out to visit the churches. First stop, Centre Church. This is the church in which I was commissioned by Bishop Ntambo as a missionary way back in 1998, and I have good memories here. The district women leaders are rehearsing for a special women's Sunday, so we get to meet some of them. We're shamed into contributing to the party fund for the Sunday celebration after worship.

I'm not terribly excited by the day's plan for touring schools and clinics and such. I've seen most of these places before and am only slightly interested in noting whether they are in better or worse shape than the last time I saw them. It turns out to be a little of both. Some sites have continued their long decline since missionary days; others have been renewed and have taken on a new life.

My interest hit bottom when we were walked around a schoolyard, and the director (principal) complained that the well was not in a good location for the students and wanted to move it 50 yards to the west. I've been riding through villages that don't have a well at all, and he wants his moved fifty yards. I'm through here.

Sunday worship is at Quatre-Vingt-Deux ("Eighty-Two") Church. Its name comes from the fact that it is located in the busy market district called Quatre-Vingt-Deux—the same reason many of our congregations in the US also have strange names. We're shown the structural problems of the building. One wall is about to collapse, and the repairs are going to be expensive.

The offerings in this worship give me some clarity on the actual state of the economy related to church finance. Not all churches do it the same way here, and I suspect that no church does it the same way every Sunday. But there are some patterns in the offerings. The offering is almost always the most joy-filled and participatory part of worship. The congregation typically dances their offerings down to offering boxes or baskets—usually two—with lots of singing. Everyone can participate, even those who have nothing to give. Opening an empty hand above the offering box is perfectly acceptable. Passing the plate, the way most churches do in the States, sometimes happens in city churches, but that is quite the exception.

During this worship, there were four offerings spread out over the whole service, and I'm not going to recount them in order. I was seated in a spot where I could watch the worshippers dance past the offering boxes. I felt a bit like Jesus in the story of the Widow's Mite, sitting in the Temple overlooking the offerings.

One offering was for the building fund. The construction committee would be meeting the following Wednesday, and all were invited to come and help make bricks. Those who would not be able to come on Wednesday were invited to contribute now in cash. A few went to the offering boxes.

There was an offering to welcome the pastors back from Annual Conference. Although the conference was in Kamina this year, pastors are given a whole month off after the conference to move to their new assignments or to take care of personal affairs. This church's two pastors are both well-liked, and the congregation was happy to have them both return. Bags of cassava, maize, and potatoes, along with chickens and bolts of fabric, salt, anything that said "welcome back," were dragged into the church. While the congregation struggles to meet the pastors' salaries, they bring these gifts with great enthusiasm. This offering happened at the close of the service, and then the church broke up into a grand party.

It's the two offerings in the middle that caught my attention.

The first was the Tithe Offering. I've been in worship in other places for the tithe offering. People bring their tithes in envelopes, and the gift is noted. The tithers may even be asked to say a word. This is not an offering done in secret.

In this church, on this Sunday, the lay leader got up and explained the tithe. He spent a good deal of time explaining it. Although I don't understand Swahili that well, I can understand tone, and this was not a nagging tone. It seemed relaxed and non-anxious; upbeat, but not cheerleader rah-rah; almost businesslike.

The choir began to sing, but nobody approached the offering boxes. The lay leader spoke a little more but not panicked. Still, no one came. The song ended, a prayer was said, and worship moved on.

It struck me that the people of this congregation tithe in real-time. No one got paid this week, so no one brought a tithe. Most people don't have a paying job, and even those who do are often not paid. People will continue to go to work every day, even when they are not being paid because they can't afford not to. Health care is tied to their employment. And there's always the hope that someday they will get back pay. Anyway, this week, no one got paid.

The next offering was the Thank Offering, an opportunity to give God thanks for the blessings of this week and for future blessings. Everyone participates. Everyone. The choir sings. The church dances. Everyone comes by the offering box, some putting in ragged, dirty bills, others opening an empty hand over the box. There are several praise testimonies telling the stories of God's grace this week.

Here's what I saw: This is where this community lives—somewhere between the Thank Offering and the Tithe Offering, somewhere between having to trust God for life's every need, and the day when they can be co-participants in building God's kingdom. The infrastructure is in place for the time when their resources will help build the church and the community. In the meantime, they will rejoice in the gifts that sustained them this week. What an amazing place to live!

Around Kamina

DAYS OF WAITING FOR Bishop Ntambo turn into weeks. We begin to look for things to do. We go out to the new Kamina Methodist University that the bishop is building.

We go out to visit the farm the bishop has developed. He has restored an old Belgian farmhouse and built a new dormitory for students to create a teaching farm.

The visit I enjoy the most is a short bicycle ride out to a small village. It should have been an unremarkable visit. There is nothing particularly unique about this village, and it has a lot in common with many of the other villages the Friendly Planet teams have visited. Maybe that's what catches my attention.

In the worship in the grass-roofed, dirt floor hut of a sanctuary, I recognize everyone. I am a stranger in this village, a first-time visitor, and yet, I feel like I know everyone already: the village chief, the pastor, the pastor's wife, the president of the Kipendano, the precocious little girl in the front row of the choir, the young man at the drum, and the younger boy trying to be like him. As people stand up and speak, I know what they are going to say before they say it. I know who is going to say what.

This is the village. This village is made up of the same people as the last fifty villages we have seen. These bicycle trips that bring us from village to village have taught me a pattern; they've taught me what to expect, what kinds of people we will meet, and how they will interact with one another. But is this a good pattern? I don't know.

Here's my question: If it takes a village to raise a child, as the African saying goes, what does it take to make a village? Please, someone, some real anthropologist, do the research and answer my question. If we knew this answer, we might know the building blocks for health and prosperity.

It takes a village to raise a child. What does it take to make a village?

On the River | The Third Tour

Finally, we can wait no longer. The bishop is still delayed in Lubumbashi, but we have to be off. Two weeks in Kamina is one week too long. We're leaving.

Kabando Dianda and Nyembo Umpungu

The air is cool, as daylight is just beginning. Our legs are fresh, and the road south is hard, smooth, and slightly downhill. The grade is almost imperceptible, except it's easier to go fast. And ride fast we do. It's exactly 100 kilometers from Kamina to Kabando Dianda. We arrive before lunch.

There's a full meal for us in Kabando Dianda, but no fuss. The district superintendent from Nyembo Umpungu has ridden his motorcycle to meet us and escort us the rest of the way to Nyembo. He's full of energy and anxious to see that we get there quickly. He has plans. I don't learn his name. Nobody uses it, and I don't ask. Everyone just calls him Baba DS.

The remaining thirty kilometers is not quite as good as the first 100, but we ride hard to keep up with our host's motorcycle. He is excited.

Nyembo is another one of those towns, like Bukama and Lubudi, where the roads are all rocks. It's hard riding, and we have to watch carefully for the rocks that could cut our tires and ruin our day.

We ride directly to the conference center that John Enright built. It is oversized for its present use; its large auditorium built for conferences is now used as a local church. It stands as a monument to indecision.

Again, I say—to the reader and myself— this book is not a history of missionaries in North Katanga. John Enright is a fascinating character, and I'm sure his life would make for a good book, but this is not that book. Someone else can write that book. However, in wandering around the remote districts of North Katanga, looking at what is left after the missionaries have gone, Nyembo Umpungu is impossible to ignore.

There is an awkwardness here. The pride of the Congolese church leaders who now run the place prevents them from directly connecting their story with the stories of the departed missionaries, but their desperation overrides their pride. There are also some backstories that I only have hints to, that I don't have enough facts to report on. Nyembo Umpungu is the catch basin of church politics and intrigue. A good novel full of sex, conspiracy, and assassination attempts could be set here. But I only have whispered rumors spoken in languages I do not understand.

Is an appointment to Nyembo-Umpumgu an opportunity or a banishment? I can't get a straight answer from the bishop. Of course, I don't ask him a straight question.

Kyungu wa Ngoy Bertin

Kyungu wa Ngoy Bertin is the new superintendent in Nyembo-Umbumgu. He's a friend who has stayed in my house in Indiana, and he is full of enthusiasm for his work. When he told me that he was going to Nyembo to be the district superintendent, I told him two things—he has a hard puzzle to solve, and he has a great house. He does. The house is missionary-grade. So many of our district superintendents live in substandard houses falling down around them. The superintendent's house in Nyembo is large, new construction, and it even has a garage if he ever got a car. Nyembo is not a place where a car would do much good. A motorcycle, though, would be good.

Nyembo is a tough nut to crack, though, for a district superintendent who inherits all the facilities that the missionaries have built up but receives no financial support from the US. The church owns all the property and all the problems.

Kyungu is excited about our arrival, a little too excited. He is introducing me to everyone as "one of us." However, it seems that no one is buying his "Bob is Congolese" statement. I'll never be one of them. It wouldn't help them if I were one of them. He's trying to sell an image that just is not selling.

His enthusiasm reminds me that there is a whole range of personalities among our leadership. A common error in development is to paint everyone with the same brush. We have to stop saying, "Congolese think this or behave this way." There is a rich diversity of opinions, skills, and behaviors like in the US.

I do get to see more of Nyembo this time than before, and the conversations are more open than before. Setting aside church politics, the church has some obvious problems.

On the River | The Third Tour

The mission station at Nyembo was built by missionaries with direct support from donors back home in Indiana and Ohio. Tractors came from the John Deere dealership in Fishers, Indiana. The sawmills came from Woodmizers in Indianapolis. But now that the missionaries have left, the supply line for parts has been cut. On the one hand, I can see how easy it would be for an American missionary to come right in here and reestablish the donor relationships and get this mission station back on its feet and running well. It's all here, and it wouldn't take but $50,000 to $100,000 in fundraising. But this is not my project, and it is not my responsibility. It is not my calling. I'm trying hard to talk myself down from the seductive temptation to be that patron of this project.

As usual, our host has delayed us a full day, hungry for the time to show us his world and his dreams, along with all the problems he is facing. I get a little annoyed at what I might call whining, but when I think about it, the problems are insurmountable and not because of laziness or ignorance. No amount of hard work or seminars on development is going to fix this. The people of Nyembo are stuck in an old model that wasn't self-sufficient even in the missionary days and has become impossible. The missionaries brought shipping containers filled with donated tractors and sawmills to set up farms and lumber mills. These never did turn a profit; the poverty is so deep. I find it remarkable that local leadership has done as well as they have without access to the missionaries' supply lines.

Kasanga

FRIENDLY PLANET'S PLANS HAVE CHANGED. Mary and the *Indiana* are not going all the way to Bukama, and they are going to pick us up at a fishing village just 16 kilometers from Nyembo. That will save us a day on the river and the high cost of port fees at Bukama.

We're off to Kasanga, the fishing village where the bicycle team will meet the boat team. Just 16 kilometers should be a quick ride, just a couple hours on the bikes.

It takes us an hour to go the first half kilometer. The trail is a narrow footpath through the forest with steep hills. Even the machetes come out to cut the way. Where the trail isn't rocks and roots, it's mud. Our motorcycle gets buried in the mud, and we fear we might have to abandon it. We've gone from traveling 130 kilometers in one day from Kamina to Nyembo to only 16 kilometers in a day from Nyembo to Kasanga.

It's mid-afternoon when we arrive. The village sits high over the river, and the view is spectacular. That great African river spread out before us!

Because I know this village is difficult to reach by road, I'm surprised by the material goods available in the marketplace—colorful new clothing, pots and pans, plastic wares. All of this new merchandise, neither second-hand nor village primitive, is coming down the river from Bukama. In the market, I meet a young man selling clothing he has made from Congolese cotton, colorful and good stuff.

On the village tour, we are taken to meet the chief of police, but there is no bureaucratic exchange of papers. Instead of being asked to produce passports, an Order of Missions, or other documents, we are greeted as welcomed guests. I can't describe the difference between the hearty handshake and photo ops we get here and sitting down at a desk and answering questions about the purpose of the visit that I've come to expect.

On the River | The Third Tour

In the evening, just before sunset, Mary and the boat arrive. So many things don't happen on time here—or don't happen at all, such as our visit with Bishop Ntambo in Kamina. There's something right about Mary's arrival at Kasanga—she arrives on time with the boat.

Mary is the leader, an unusual position for a woman in this part of Congo. Mary's leadership is a surprise to me. The *Indiana's* boat crew could have brought the boat to us; instead, they brought the boat and Mary. I can't quite describe it: it's not exactly a class system, but Mary has something that overrides the expected division of labor by gender. I particularly watch Éléphant. His body language and good-natured, instant obedience to anything she orders tell me that he has no problem being led by a woman. At least, he has no problem being led by Mary.

We attend the obligatory church meeting. In the usual pattern, we gather for worship during which choirs sing, and we are introduced as visitors. We each say a bit, but not too much. I'm aware that my speaking is taken as a commitment to help out here. It's tough to greet people and keep them at a distance so as not to become their missionary.

The pastor and his wife pose for photos with me, and I recognize them from conferences. They're middle-aged and carry comfortable confidence in their leadership. I'm impressed by the pig project they show me. Again, I think that this small, isolated village has a lot going for it. I'm also thinking that wherever we go, we find these isolated communities that surprise me with their visionary leadership. I'm beginning to craft a saying. "We have plenty of excellent leaders. Each of these leaders is this close (show hands close together) to succeeding. Yet, the overall failure rate is 100%." I'm becoming convinced that the place to invest our help is in this leadership. Investing doesn't mean leadership workshops. While there is a need for content learning, knowledge is not what is holding these leaders back. They can't break the cycle of their poverty. They perform heroically within their poverty, but they just can't break out. This is the puzzle. And it doesn't mean leadership from the top down. This layer of leadership right at the district and village level seems to be ready to flourish with just the right support and help.

Later, a bed is made for me in a small depot, and I have a good night of sound sleep among the chickens and bags of meal. The bike ride is over. Tomorrow morning, we get on the boat and float two days down the Congo River to Mulongo.

KASANGA

In the morning, we are up early, getting all our gear ready. I haven't seen the boat yet, but I trust that it's somewhere safe. Mary directs the boat crew to carry away all the gear the bike team has been traveling with. Everything, including my bags and bicycle, will be loaded on the boat. It will take a little time for them to get it all packed, so we take one more walk through the village.

Children are walking to school in uniforms, blue trousers or skirts and white shirts or blouses. They all have new backpacks, with the logo of some program, and I ask. The backpacks have been provided by the Ministry of Education.

What makes this village special?

A considerable crowd meets us at the river, and it's even difficult to make our way through to get to the boat. There it is: the *UM Indiana*, painted Colts blue and white. The boat crew has not only kept the boat in good shape, but they have also made some improvements on it since I last saw it. That is pleasing. Instead of watching an asset depreciate, I'm watching it appreciate.

The boat fills up with our bicycle team, the boat crew that Mary brought, and a few local United Methodists who need a ride downriver or who are enjoying being a part of whatever it is we're doing.

This is a good day. There is singing in the air, literally—the boatload of people is singing. The village has turned out to wave goodbye. The scene reminds me of so many moments of departure in classic photos and films. The whole village is standing on the edge of the water, waving to the outsiders, grass-roofed huts behind them. I get my camera out, sit on the forecastle, and take pictures until we are out of range.

On the river, Mary is in charge: she's the Chief of Mission and the Chief Medical Officer—and the Cook. While she has risen to the rank of the undisputed head—there is no indication that anyone challenges her right to be the chief—she still picks up the pan and knife and cleans the chicken for dinner. The men on this boat have no problem doing "women's work," like cooking, but whether she can't shake the traditional role, or she doesn't trust the men to do the task while she is present, Mary is in the bow of the boat cooking the meal. I laugh to myself at the sight of the captain doing a job so low in the hierarchy. That didn't happen in my Navy days.

Éléphant is in the stern steering and smiling. It's a great day to be on the river.

It's going to take two days to get to Mulongo. Since we still have no lights on the boat, we'll have to pull up for the night. There's a boat station at Kalombo, like a train station, only for riverboats. The building is abandoned and in ruins. Whatever commerce happened here, it has been gone for decades. We pull in anyway.

The abandoned building isn't hospitable, so we set up tents. It's trying to rain and seems like it will rain all night, so we pitch our tents under a new shelter that has been put up as a small market. The ground is hard, and the sleep will not be restful because of the heat and mosquitoes. But it's still about the grandest adventure you'd ever want to be on.

Reading *War and Peace*

CAN'T READ ON A bicycle, but you can on a boat. I have a lot of time to read. Slow boat to Mulongo.

Why not read *War and Peace*? On my Nook, it is 4,000 pages.

It's not at all what I expected. What a soap opera! It's addicting, like reading candy.

But I know that Tolstoy is serious. I've read *The Kingdom of God Is Within You*, a book that comes from a series of correspondences between Tolstoy and William Lloyd Garrison. Tolstoy was a huge fan of Garrison. My takeaway from their exchange was that you can't buy enough guns to enforce peace. Peace must be built at the village level. Only when all children go to school, are fed, and have a home can peace exist. This isn't a utopian idea—this is what it takes to have the kind of community foundation that prevents war. Well-fed, well-housed, well-educated children are not the result of peace but rather the cause. You have it backward if you think that once we have peace, we can build schools. War is not stopped at the front through victory, but neither is it stopped at the peace table. It is only stopped at the village level.

This leads me to think that the real work of peace is first preemptive and that it strategically has to be built well back of the front lines of fighting, out of the immediate conflict zone. We are in exactly the right spot.

Also, Tolstoy was not a proponent of the "Great Man" theory of history, the idea that history is made by remarkable individuals. In *War and Peace*, Napoleon is not creating history. He is the creation of the stories of many different people in many different countries from many different layers of society. Even though *War and Peace* is about Russia's War with Napoleon, it is not about Napoleon.

I ponder what that means for Congo. The possibility is that the great men—and they still are mostly men—who sit in parliament in Kinshasa, board rooms in Brussels, or peace talks in Geneva have less to do with the future of the Congo than do the stories of the thousands of villages in these remote places.

When I get to the final page of *War and Peace,* the trip is not yet over. I want the book to go on. I start again.

Mulongo to Manono

ONE OF THE GOALS I have for 2012 is to get back to Manono. It was Manono I took off for in 1995, abandoning my daughter and her teenage friends to total strangers in a strange land, leaving them to get themselves back to the United States. Well, not complete strangers; I left them in the care of the conference staff. Still, not my best parenting. It was in Manono that Ntambo said, "This is the best thing we have done in 30 years," after a missionary had said, "This is a nice thing you have done for them," when we distributed 50 new bicycles to pastors. (I still meet pastors who tell me that they were there and that they received one of those bicycles.) It was in Manono in 1991 and again in 1995 that I was taken out to see a mission to a Twa group.

Manono is almost exactly 100 kilometers by road from Mulongo. We could cut the riding down to 40 kilometers by taking the boat downriver to Muymba, then getting on our bikes there, but we'll take the land route.

Mumba and I take a couple young men from the boat crew to accompany us. By this time, Mumba has become a monster on the bike. He rides hard and fast, and I have trouble keeping up and find myself exhausted by trying to. It's hot.

Before we get to Ngoya, the major intersection of the road where when we turn left to head north to Manono, we leave the road for a path through the forest, a shortcut. The riding gets technical, but the pace stays up.

In the forest, we come upon what is, for me, the discovery of the trip. It's a large camp of miners with the look and feel of a camp of Irish Travelers or maybe Roma. Men, women, and children, whole families, whole extended families. There are women doing laundry, women cooking, women with babies at their breasts, children playing, and men and women working hard in the creek. They're shoveling mud into sluices made of tree bark, sifting for gold, copper, coltan, and diamonds. It's hot and hard work.

No soldiers are guarding the camp, and I find that strange since we've seen soldiers at other mining operations. We are greeted with smiles. When I pull out my camera and gesture the question, "Can I take your picture?" people are happy to stop and pose.

In the middle of nowhere, deep in the forest, in the "heart of darkness," is this community of nomads digging in the mud of the forest floor for rare minerals. They sweat in the unbearable—for me—heat, and yet at the same time, they are doing everything else that life requires. They might be the poorest, hardest-working people on the planet.

This is where it all begins. The minerals dug out of the mud in this forest camp by these poor folk will eventually become a laptop, a cell phone, or an electronic game. This is where your smartphone comes from.

I have no idea what they get paid for this work, but nothing about this scene suggests they're earning a living wage. I'm guessing that they get paid for what they find, so their lives are pulled forward more by hope than by reality.

I can't get over the fact that I've just ridden a bicycle so deep into the African forest that I have been shown something that not very many—if any—other white people will ever see. I've seen the very belly of the industrial manufacturing beast. I'll ride on to Manono, but these hard-working people will stay here. They'll be here tomorrow. This poverty is their life. There is no future but a repeat of today. They will never escape this reality. They will not be able to fly home from this experience and recover in air-conditioned comfort.

It's not my pity that is stirred; it's my sense of what's fair. With their labor under the burning sun, these mining families will produce the elements that will become the electronic toys of mind-numbed middle-class consumers all over the world and fill the bank accounts of the uber-wealthy of New York, Shanghai, and Dubai. People in the States tend to think of Africa's poor as primitives suffering under the poverty of their own ignorance. The people doing this work suffer under the poverty created by an exploitative global system. The only thing this picture lacks is the bullwhips. But what sticks in my head is the sight of whole families camped, doing ordinary family things, in the midst of this brutal labor.

Back on the main road to Manono, we pick up the pace. We'll arrive in no time. This is going to be a quick morning's ride. It is challenging to keep up, but I'm thrilled with this fast pace until one of our riders pulls up lame. He is a young man from the boat crew who has not had the experience on the bicycle required for this length of ride. I feel for him. I know his problem. He has jumped on a bicycle someone else has been riding and has not adjusted the saddle height for himself. At this point in the ride, his knees are screaming. He can't go any further. We give him permission to go back at his own pace. No shame. At least, we don't want him to feel shame.

In times like these, I question my choice not to give the team direction on bicycling skills. In trying not to be the white know-it-all, I fail to pass along simple things that I know, like how important it is to get the saddle height right if you're going to ride all day.

Here's a lesson: content education is important. People don't know things until they learn them. The puzzle is how to impart content knowledge without destroying local knowledge. For me, the key is taking the time to listen for local knowledge before teaching what I know. I'm actually good at this, possibly too good. First, I do listen with respect for local knowledge, and I do stay out of the way of local leadership in the teaching of content, but to a fault. I've forgotten that I know a lot about cycling and bicycles, not because I'm white, but because I've spent years learning about cycling and bicycles. There are other things I know, as well—the Bible, theology, leadership, even some auto mechanics.

I failed this young man in his first long-distance riding experience by not helping him sort out his bicycle before we left. It's easy to assume that everyone here is a strong rider and would first adjust the seat height, or at least complain that they didn't like the way this bicycle felt.

It's also important not to paint a whole culture with one brush. There are those who know; there are those who don't know. A huge mistake westerners make here is thinking that all Congolese know or don't know the same things. I ask young people about the trees, and they say, "I don't know." I didn't ask this rider about his cycling skills, and I should have.

Entering the Manono District

I NEVER KNOW the threat level. I have never felt unsafe. We are in a war zone, or more accurately, a peace-keeping zone. There is real rebel shooting action going on to the north of us, way north. There is Mai-Mai activity on the Red Road to the south of us. But we have never been in danger. At least, I don't think we have. When we cross into the Mitwaba District, we enter the red zone, at least a level up from where we have been. Military activity is more visible. There is now military activity on the Red Road, where we have been operating, but we've swung wide of that threat. When we cross this line, we're really in the war zone. And it doesn't take long to know it.

The first village inside the Manono District is all abuzz. There is some kind of political rally happening. A stage is being set up for an opposition party leader to speak to the crowd. And it's a big crowd.

U.N. troops are there managing the crowd. They're not being heavy-handed. They do seem to be a non-anxious presence, but they are there to control the crowd and keep this political demonstration from going ballistic, literally.

We enter the village on our bicycles, and I'm looking forward to a break. The good shade is in the villages. There's always some kind of hospitality to break up the ride, but Mumba looks concerned and indicates that we will not break until well after the village. He leads us straight and deliberately through the crowd—eyes ahead, no eye contact. We must be the most curious group of tourists making our way through the festival, but no one pays any attention to us. Whatever is happening is more important than the strange arrival of a white man on a bicycle.

The road through the village goes straight into the thick of the crowd. In the thick of the thick is the U.N. Peacekeeper commander. Our eyes meet. He doesn't flinch or change his stance. He directs us with the smallest of motions to move on through. He doesn't need us in the mix. Usually, this

Entering the Manono District

would have been a time of document checking and questions about what we were doing in the war zone. But not today. He has an important mission, and it doesn't include us.

There was a kind of recognition. Both of us are outsiders: he is Black, and I am white, but we're the same. This peacekeeper, who is probably from Benin, is no more a part of this village than I am.

We get on through, and it's several kilometers before Mumba thinks it is safe to stop. Like I said, I have no idea what the threat level is. I don't want to overstate it and get credit for being in more danger than we have been, but the truth is, I don't know.

A couple hours later, the truck full of U.N. soldiers passes us on their way back to Manono.

Manono

ON THE OUTSKIRTS OF TOWN, we find a stretch of tarmac. We haven't seen a paved road since Kamina. Granted, it's mostly in sad shape, and it's like one of those post-nuclear war apocalyptic movies; underneath is the evidence of a former civilization. On the surface is the reminder that whatever created this civilization is long gone and not coming back.

As we enter the town, I'm looking for war damage. It's there, but now the burned-out buildings are covered in jungle. The jungle is healing itself.

We arrive in Manono so early that the welcoming committee is still forming. I have to grin as we wait for church leaders to get their act together. It's just a bit funny. Nothing is wrong. We just got here faster than anyone expected. I'm thinking that with a group of riders as strong and as determined as Mumba, we could get around these districts pretty fast. We're just now learning how to do this well, and the three-year tour is almost over.

We're shown what's left of one of our United Methodist churches, an old sunbaked brick building with a grass roof. The walls are only half standing, and the roof is only a memory. It is sad. I can't tell if it has been damaged by the war or just by years of weather and neglect. They tell me that this is the church that Lena Eschtruth built while doing medical outreach work in this region in the '80s. This town is going to try to connect me to the story of the early missionaries. That's their hook. This is different from other places where, even when we were standing in missionary-built buildings, the missionaries were not mentioned. We're going to be shown a couple more of these churches, but as I said, I'm not sure that we're looking at war damage, as much as looking at a missionary-started church that hasn't seen any real work since the missionaries left.

This is a UN town. The streets are swarming with white UN trucks. Back in the '90s, this area was a ghost town of old storefronts built in the

'40s and closed when the mine closed in the '70s, but the old European downtown merchant section is alive again. Shops are full of stock running over onto the sidewalks—mountains of bags of flour and rice, stacks and stacks of water, Cokes, and beer; all kinds of sundries. Sundries of sundries. This is a Boom Town again. I wonder what will happen when the troops go home. Bust. Will Manono become a ghost town again?

We ride past the old compound of the missionaries Ken and Lorraine Enright, which has been commandeered by the UN Peacekeeping troops. The remains of the old house are still visible; bomb damage exposes most of the inside to the outside. The compound has become a military garrison surrounded by a high barbed-wire fence.

We make the required visit to immigration and to the territorial administrator, who has one scolding question for me: "Why have the United Methodists abandoned their people?"

At the center of Manono, we rode around the giant roundabout that circles the Catholic cathedral, the city's largest and most important building. We're told that this cathedral's roof was bombed off. The Catholics rebuilt it immediately after the war, and it has been restored to its original cathedral-scale beauty. No wonder the territorial administrator wanted to know what had happened to the United Methodists. It sure looks like we just abandoned our people. None of our churches have been rebuilt.

That got me thinking about polity, that is, church governance and structure. Clearly, United Methodist polity is different from Catholic polity. We aren't organized in the same way, and funding doesn't come in the same way. It must be confusing to a local community to compare the Catholic response to the United Methodist non-response.

Bishop Ntambo, along with Taylor, made a visit to Manono in 2005, immediately after the war. The ceasefire was in effect, UN troops occupied Manono, and Taylor traveled with the Bishop on special papers to visit inside the war zone. The town of Manono was totally destroyed in the war. Taylor saw the devastation firsthand before the town got cleaned up, but that pastoral visit never translated into material assistance to rebuild. Around that time, United Methodists were asked to send money for rebuilding after many disasters, but not this one. Why not?

The more I reflected on polity, the more I was drawn to see a polity perception gap. The missionaries who came to Manono had come based on their own sense of call. There was no general church strategy. The missionaries raised their own salaries and money for their projects by traveling from congregation to congregation in the United States and pitching their cause. Yes, they were employed by the General Board of Global Ministries, but GBGM served as a human resources management agency. The actual funding came from individual local congregations and was given directly to the accounts of these missionaries. A fund made sure missionaries were paid even if they did not raise enough, but some missionaries, like the Enrights, raised far more than they cost.

So, when the missionaries left, the Americans involved only saw an individual missionary, or couple, retiring, dying, or moving on to something else. What the community, however, saw was The United Methodist Church leaving.

This polity perception gap is demonstrated in the signage. The sign at a United Methodist church in America will say something like "Shelburn United Methodist Church." Some will say, "First United Methodist Church," or "Trinity United Methodist Church." Some new church starts will say something like "The Gathering," with "a United Methodist Community" (in small print). Anyway, the primary identity is of the local congregation. Although delegates elected to General Conference and seminary-trained pastors are taught the polity handed down from Mr. Wesley and perfected in the *Book of Discipline*, the more common perception of United Methodist polity in the pews is of a federation of congregations who participate in the shared mission voluntarily. And our mission practices reflect this perceived polity. Any mission activity is engaged in only as individual congregations (or people) decide to participate on their own. There is no general missional strategy. Even general church missional initiatives like No More Malaria have to raise money by appealing to congregations and individuals. Apportionments (denominational taxes) cover only the bare-bones structural operating costs. All actual missions are done with money raised for particular projects.

In the Congo, however, the sign on the church says, "*L'Église Méthodiste Unie*," French for "The United Methodist Church." The local congregation is identified in small print below. There's a huge "cross and flame"—the corporate logo of The United Methodist Church, at one time, the second most recognized corporate logo in Africa after Coca-Cola. Times have changed, and other corporate logos (Apple, Microsoft, Zando's Chicken) are more familiar now, but the point is that each local congregation identifies itself with this shared global corporation. When the community looks at that sign, they see a strong global partner. Nobody thinks that this congregation is strong enough to deliver the needed help on its own, but everybody knows that The United Methodist Church is one of the strongest and wealthiest churches in the world.

The practical outgrowth of this United Methodist polity focusing on individual action is that if no missionary raises money for a project, the project—the school, the clinic, the evangelism—is not funded. Similarly, there is no support for the regular, day-to-day, ongoing work of the church and the pastor. When the missionary leaves, the local congregation or district does not have the resources to maintain the work of that school or clinic started by the missionary. The project was never self-supporting; the missionary raised the needed funds from congregations in America. The local church leaders left with the responsibility of running these projects do not have access to that funding stream. Yes, there is a catalog of projects available to American churches where the project can be featured, but the reality is that if your project doesn't have an advocate pitching it—a missionary visiting churches in the US—it doesn't get funding.

So, when the missionaries left Manono, it felt like The United Methodist Church was abandoning it.

Mission and Abandonment

Joseph writes:

During all the time I spent with Bob riding our bicycles, my first joy was that Bob was bringing a new vision of mission. Compared to what we knew as missionaries, as mission, what Bob was trying to bring was really, really different. Before, missionaries were considered as patrons. Missionaries had been coming to different parts of our episcopal area, bringing their own programs, their own projects. If you visit North Katanga District, you will see many good projects were abandoned. If you ask people what happened, they say that it was the missionary's project, and when the missionaries left, he left with his projects. There was no one who could continue, so the missionary was on one side with his project, and the congregation, the community, was there, watching what the missionary was doing.

With Bob, we've been doing deep listening everywhere we've been visiting people. We have the time to hear people's joy. On the other side, we have been hearing their fear, their struggles. If people have a problem, they have a part to play in the solution to their problem. That's what Bob had been trying to teach through deep listening. Visiting with Bob was giving a new hope to the church.

Shabana concurs:

In my safari with Baba Bob, I have learned much of what a mission should be like.

First, I have understood that the ministry is to be available and present in the area of your mission. Leaders and missionaries should not make themselves too busy, even for their own ministry, as an excuse not to feed the sheep of our Lord. Jesus asks Peter in the book of John three times, saying, "Do you love me?" And the finishing task was, "Go and feed my sheep." How can we feed God's sheep while we are very busy people as politicians? How can we feed the sheep we don't even want to meet? To go, in Jesus's perspective, means leaving our position to move towards the sheep and not making the sheep come to where we are.

Most of the church leaders are busy with trips abroad, with conferences here and there, but cannot take even one month a year visiting churches, especially those in the remote areas. And when it comes that they visit some of the churches, they just stay for one day.

Mission is to stay with the people, in the real sense of doing as they do, so as to understand their problems and learn a solution in that same community. Mission is not to provide money, clothes, and healthcare, which only help for a while; it is to come up with development ideas together with the same communities for sustainable projects, which will help even after the mission is closed.

It is sad that when you get to any place where there was a Methodist mission, you'll see traces only but no mission enhancement. You will be shocked to visit Manono today and see the agricultural project that missionaries had settled in the past and how it is abandoned now. In the same way, one can visit Nyembo Center, Kanene, Mwanza Seya and realize the magnitude of these missions.

Three Water Projects

WE'RE STANDING IN THE yard of the flagship United Methodist Church in Manono. It's the old missionary-built church, and its solid construction has survived weather and wars. The church building needs attention, but from ten yards away, it looks good.

We take a walk around the yard. Besides the church itself, there are a clinic and two schools. The nurse who staffs the clinic met us in his white lab coat and gave us a tour of the space: a central receiving area with two small rooms on the side, one room for patient consultation and the other for his bed. He proudly shows me his microscope, carefully opening the wooden box it is kept in. That is it. There are no meds and no patients. He asks for money for medicines and for his salary.

The building that housed the primary school has been mostly destroyed in a fire—arson, not war-related. Charred remains of a grass roof still litter the cement floor, and only one end wall is standing.

The secondary school is in good shape and is functioning, with classrooms filled with students and teachers at work as we toured. A young man was brought out of a classroom to greet us. His legs were shriveled up, and he scooted himself on the dirt with his strong arms. He did not present himself to us as a beggar but instead greeted us with self-confidence. The principal stated the young man's need for a hand crank tricycle and a scholarship for school fees. The need for a scholarship for school fees is universal, and the need for hand-crank tricycles is common to every village. Polio? Early childhood accidents? War? I don't know the causes, but every village has at least one person who needs personal transportation.

As we pass between the church and the burned-out primary school, I stop at a covered well. Our hosts weren't even going to mention it. "Oh, it's dry," someone says. This well was dug in the days of the missionaries, maybe in the '60s.

Three Water Projects

When we get to the corner of the secondary school, I notice a standing, silo-shaped concrete cistern designed to collect water from the roof. I also see that the sections of sheet metal guttering hung along the edge of the roof are disconnected. There is no way the runoff from the roof is making it to the cistern. Mumba tries to turn the handle on the spigot, but it won't budge. He asks questions about the design of the cistern. It seems to him that the spigot was placed too high, so that much of the water would always be unavailable. Neither Mumba nor I know the first thing about cistern construction, and our ignorance is on display, but no one there can answer our simplest questions about a water collection machine with no moving parts. How does this thing work? Why is it not working? The principal of the school is a smart guy. He's not an engineer, but he should have been instructed in the care and management of this water system. All we find out is that it had been built by an Irish NGO. It can't be more than five years old—and already it is not working.

Across the road, we see the kind of water pump becoming ubiquitous in Africa. The boys are pumping, and there is no water coming out; it's like a strange kind of playground equipment. I ask about the pump. It was put there by the UN when the peacekeepers arrived. After less than five years, it's not working, and no one knows why.

Here's the lesson for today: it is not sufficient for the community to own the project—the community must own the problem.

This is one of our most important lessons, so it bears repeating: *It is not sufficient for a community to own the project. It must first own the problem.*

Breaking Rules to Connect
to the Past

WE RIDE OUT TO the edge of town to some old mine company housing. These are solid small brick homes, old and tired, worn down by seasons of rain and sun. To my American eyes, it has the look of a squatter town, but I know that these homes are coveted and come through connections with the mining company, even though the mine is no longer functioning. These mines still have a skeleton structure that operates off the ever-shrinking assets.

There's a well-built church here with what looks like a new metal roof. We're told that Ken Enright had built the church and had recently donated the roofing. I think it looks too recent to have been built by the Enrights, but I don't argue with them.

We go to see the school that missionaries built. It's big, with two major buildings the size of large commercial truck garages. In its day, this was a first-rate high school for auto mechanics and electricians, but it was pretty well gutted during the war, stripped of anything of worth, and used to garrison troops. There's still war graffiti—mostly "Rambo" stuff—on the walls.

More recently, one classroom has been roofed and painted by an Irish NGO. It looks nice, but it is still an empty shell. They need desks, books, tools, and all the things a class for auto mechanics and electricians would require. Remarkably, there is a large enrollment here for class this day.

I break my rule and ask about the ministry to the Twa, the local indigenous people. "Oh, that's going well." But there's no invitation to go see it. It is 17 kilometers away, but I get the feeling that it's not going that well, and there's no urgency to get me out to see it.

Sunday comes, and we have worship in the old mission church. Surprise! The young man who talked with me under the tree back in 1995 is here. I am so thrilled to meet him that I break yet another rule and ask him to be my translator. My rule is that I use pastors from our team, not English teachers we pick up in town. His poor job of communicating the ideas developed by our team reminds me why I have that rule, but I thought that being able to tell the story of that first time we had met there in Manono was worth it.

Manono to Kanteba

Aha!

THE DISTRICT SUPERINTENDENT OF the neighboring Kanteba District has organized a visit for us. From Manono, we ride only about 15 kilometers east into the Kanteba District and to the village of Kanteba, just outside of the Manono District.

Kanteba is larger than a typical village but not as large as Manono. It's more like a suburb of Manono. In the colonial days, it was a company town for mine workers in the tin mine on the east side of Manono.

Scouts meet us on the outskirts of the village and form a small but enthusiastic parade to march us in. The scouts stay with us the whole day as security, even though the threat level here is almost zero.

A lunch is served at a church member's home, an old office building converted into a house. The ground around the building has washed away to the point that it takes a big step up to reach the first step of the porch, pretty much like every colonial-era building everywhere here. The living room (converted office) is enormous. We sit around two large tables and enjoy the meal. The district superintendent brings out a box of electronic equipment that turns out to be a ham radio lacking the microphone to make it functional. He complains, Mumba with him, that they have been given a useless radio. If the radio worked, and even if there were a microphone, it would still lack an antenna and electricity. Still, if the radio worked, the district would have a communications link through the pilot. As it is, it may take months for the district to get news from the conference. The problem here is that this district does not have cell phone coverage. This situation is more common in remote districts than I had realized. I thought there was cell coverage just about everywhere, but not so. I'm learning.

Outside, in the yard, is a grain mill that is also not working.

Missionaries Ken and Lorraine Enright had an active ministry here in the 1990s. The last real help to the village came as a gift from Ken Enright for school roofing before he died in 2006. We're taken to the school to see the new roof, now several years old, and hear an appeal for more money to finish the rest of the school. The more I learn about Ken and Lorraine Enright, the more impressed I am with their work. They were doing great things, and they left a hole in this world that has yet to be filled. I'm being courted to replace them, but I know I can't be them. Truth is, it is inviting, and I could love settling in a village like this one to be their missionary. But that resident missionary system is not the answer.

We sit in a large circle and enjoy the worship led by two choirs. I'm sitting directly opposite the group of scouts, and I'm struck by their posture and attentiveness. I pull out my camera and begin shooting. I make sure that I take pictures of the choirs, as well, and at least point the camera at the dignitaries.

The district superintendent talks, but everyone knows we are filling the time waiting for the chief to arrive. Nothing important is going to happen until he arrives, and we're going to wait until either the chief comes or Jesus comes, whichever is first.

The chief may not even come. This is a pretty remote village, one of the hundreds not on any map. After the Enright's departure, it is unlikely that any other outsider is ever going to pass this way again, except today and me.

When the chief does come, I'm impressed with him. He's not old, but not young either. He's eloquent and poised. His words are wise, and his leadership sound. Even though the other leaders in the village are making pitches to me as a potential patron, he is speaking of self-actualization. His understanding is not the understanding driving the official leadership of this country, but it is not that rare. I hear this kind of talk in more places than not. It's in the grassroots, just not at the top. And here is the frustration: The big NGOs and the general agencies of the Church are working with the top leaders, the ones who are still looking for patrons.

I could work with this chief. I would love to work with this chief. I could settle in this village, and we could build schools and clinics and churches and markets and cure diseases and create businesses. Together, we could transform a village in poverty into a model village of prosperity. All the pieces are here, including the leadership.

We take a group walk through the village. This is the more common, unsexy story of what the war has done. All previous housing stock was leveled, and the replacements are sad-looking huts. I'm not the only one who sees this. The district superintendent takes me to his house, his hut, to show me the sad state of his existence.

We walk past a well whose steel pump has been broken off. The inscription in the concrete base: "International Red Cross 2005." I figure that this well is the final act of rebuilding after the war and the last time an international aid organization will come through here. Ever.

This is where I have my "aha!" moment, my "Eureka!" my revelation, my enlightenment. It comes from something I've known since 1995 but am only now seeing in real village life. It starts in my gut but goes to my brain, and I can almost say it out loud. Not quite, but almost. It's still in the implicit phase, but I know that I know it.

I was told a long time ago that it takes approximately 5% of the population to run the mines. Because mining is an extractive industry that removes things from the community, companies put little back into the community. Factoring in the military, government, and a rising middle class of professionals, doctors, lawyers, this leaves over 80% of the population that is non-essential to the economy. In a village like this one, where the mine has closed, and there is nothing else to replace it, the number approaches 100%. If the only focus of the economy is mining, and as much as 95% of the population does not participate in that industry, then the vast majority of the people are not essential to the economy. That is why ten percent of a country's population can die, and no one besides the grieving family members is impacted. The people in villages like Kanteba are on their own, and there are thousands of villages like Kanteba.

This explains why the most common theme I hear in village after village is the feeling of abandonment.

What to do? It's clear that aid projects, no matter how noble and needed they appear from the outside looking in, are not working and won't work. Dig a well, and in three years, the pump will be broken. Give a bed net, and it will be used for fishing. Donate roofing sheets, and next year, you'll be asked for more. There is no end to the help required to rescue people outside of a country's economic system.

How do we bring them into the economy, or how do we create a new economy that includes them?

For this village to make it, somehow it has to be seen as essential to the economy, someone's economy. Any development attempt that does not include the people of this village in a working economy will fail. I'm having a vision of adding one more aspect to Bishop Ntambo's vision of the ideal church and parsonage. Besides the clinic and school, add a general store.

Ride Back from Manono

We've been staying in the home of a church member. It's broken but safe and comfortable. There's a bathtub, and I was provided with a bucket of hot water each day for my bath. It has been a small luxury. As long as I have bottled water for brushing my teeth, I'm good to go.

We leave Manono at daybreak. Breakfast is served in the dark. Candles used to be the common source of light where there was no electricity, but nowadays, battery-powered LED lamps from China are standard. Breakfast is bread—loaves cut down the middle lengthwise with a big slab of Rama brand margarine for flavor and energy. Product labeling in Africa boasts of energy content rather than warning of calorie content. The numbers are the same, but the attitude is different. Sometimes, the margarine tastes like gasoline, but most of the time, I could live on bread and margarine, and Rama's yellow tub has become a familiar sight.

We all fill our water bottles and make our last-minute bike checks. We say goodbyes to all who are awake for our departure. Another familiar sight is the shell of an old Land Rover in the driveway. There are lots of these around, all their usable, sellable parts removed, leaving only the aluminum shell remaining. Land Rovers are different from the Chevy trucks rusting away in the villages because Land Rovers don't rust.

We ride out through the sand streets of Manono. Sand streets make for slow riding, but slow riding means that I really see things. I notice a young boy wearing a t-shirt advertising the Vacation Bible School program of Sunrise Baptist Church. I once pastored a Sunrise United Methodist Church. The kids, and adults, wear t-shirts with all kinds of messages. A lot of church hand-me-downs, a lot of over-stocks. I can tell which quarterbacks are no longer trending in the States by the appearance of their jerseys here. Then, there are the shirts with crude messages that the wearer is clearly unaware of and the shirts with products that the wearer is clearly unfamiliar with. Pastors lead worship in Jack Daniels shirts. You have to smile.

When we hit that short section of tarmac, we pick up the pace and ride past the bombed-out homes, past the freshly painted Jehovah's Witness Kingdom Hall, past the auto mechanics' school. We make one last stop before leaving Manono.

As per usual, it's hard to get out of town. The local leadership can't let us go without one last pitch for their projects. Who knows? It could be—will be—years before another missionary comes through here. In fact, I don't think they understand that this is probably it for missionaries. If their plan is to recruit a missionary to come and live in Manono, they need to find a new plan. But pitch the plan they do, and if I didn't have a wife at home who refuses to move overseas, I would be an easy mark for their pitch.

The district superintendent wants us to see the district farm, which occupies a lot of acreage on the outskirts of town. The old farmhouse is overgrown by the jungle. Manono's climate approaches the standards for a rainforest, so the vegetation is actually jungle. This had been, of course, the farm of a missionary. They tell me his name, but he was well before my time. The district superintendent is able to keep the fields in production, growing maize, melons, and vegetables, but he has no money for restoring the buildings. They are particularly proud of an irrigated rice field, their newest project. I notice a couple women working in the fields, small and shy. Mulongo confirms that they are Twa.

I could live here, have a farm in Africa, just like *Out of Africa*. A kind of magic draws white people to Africa—the fantasy of living in a big house in a beautiful rural location, with lots of servants for the manual labor. Well, that fantasy draws a particular personality of white people. I'm probably reading too much Conrad.

We ride past the old tin mine, its rusting superstructure announcing the end of the colonial era. The Belgians left 50 years ago, and it has taken this long for their presence to fade into the wild.

The road is hard-packed dirt, and the riding is fast. The sun is hot, and I could use a break, but Mumba is not going to stop. I relish the sections of the road that have been washed out. Even though they are dry, they offer a terrain change that slows us. We hit one section that is more like one of those dirt bike racecourses. Americans actually pay extra for this kind of fun. But it's hot.

At 30 kilometers, we find the shortcut path into the forest that takes us through the mining camp. We meet a couple uniformed mineworkers on motorcycles coming the other way. They are wearing coveralls and hard hats, the signs of a real job. They're not high ranking, but we don't spend any time in the camp now that the supervisors have spotted us. We ride straight through with waves and smiles.

We pop out of the forest on the road to Mulongo. I hate this road. I hate the sand. My Cannondale touring bike does not have the tire width for sand. I'm constantly frustrated with the pattern: ride a few yards, get stuck in the deep sand, get off, push, find a hard spot, ride a few yards, get stuck, repeat. I hate this.

The Zambike mountain bikes fare a bit better, but even they struggle, and eventually, we are all walking and cursing the sand. Well, I don't really know if the others are cursing, but no one is saying happy things.

Our solution is to ride along the edge of the road, where it is still hard, but it's only six inches wide and right against the brush of the forest. I foolishly begin to pick up speed. Just as I lose focus on riding and begin to daydream—*crash!* I'm totally unaware, but what has happened is a stump of a small tree has grabbed my rear pannier, and, while my bicycle came to a full and sudden stop, I did not.

Back as midshipmen at the Naval Academy, my roommate Don and I took a P.E. course in hand-to-hand combat taught by a Navy Seal lieutenant. He spent most of the class time training us in the art of falling. The training must have stuck because flying over the handlebars, I tuck my lead arm and roll out over that shoulder. However, that is about all the control I can muster. Out-of-body, as if in slow motion, I observe my head and left side slam onto the ground. There is nothing I can do to stop it, and I just watch it happen. Of course, I am not wearing a helmet.

I lay there on the ground, catching my breath. I don't think I'm hurt too bad, but I'm not sure if I'm fully conscious. My inner right thigh hit something hard going over the handlebars, and that hurts. The back side of my right ribs is in some pain, but I don't think anything is broken. By now, my colleagues have reached me and are anxious to help. I ask them to just let me lie there for a bit, but I assure them that I'm OK. I stay on the ground until I've regained my vision, sense, and breath.

This has been my greatest fear: that I'd be in a bike wreck that would break an arm, and we'd be too far from help. This wreck comes almost as a relief. I wrecked. No bones broken, I think. The bike is not permanently damaged, although the front rack will never be straight again. My glasses are badly bent and will have to be replaced when I get back home. If it had been a medical emergency, Dr. Serge would be only a cell phone call and 40 kilometers away. This was my worst-case scenario, and I survived. Good wreck.

The incident slows us down, and we're not going to get to Mulongo at our record pace. The day is getting longer. What started out as a sprint is turning into a marathon. We're going to have to take a break. Éléphant surprises us, showing up on his motorcycle. He has come out to meet us and escort us the rest of the way. I guess, if the wreck had been more serious, he would have arrived as an angel sent by God. Even so, he is a welcome sight.

He has set up a break for us at a hut along the road, under a shade tree. Éléphant has spotted a couple bats hanging high up in the tree. I get out my camera and long-range lens and snap a few shots.

Éléphant has brought us water and biscuits. We take a long break to drink and cool down. My head's going to be fine, I think. But how would I know in this heat? My leg is sore, but I'm sure nothing is broken. There's a bruise on my rib cage that might be serious. I'll let Dr. Serge look at it when we get to Mulongo.

This world is so bizarre. Amazing. We're sitting there under this tree in the middle of nowhere, on the road to Mulongo, and a doctor on a motorcycle rides up. He knows Éléphant, and Éléphant knows him. He's carrying an aluminum cold box on the back of the motorcycle, the kind they use to carry vaccines for rural health initiatives. He has cold drinks in the box. He offers us a cold bottle of water. It's like the ice cream truck. I wish he had an ice cream bar. I decline—I have plenty of water, and having colder water isn't going to be that much better. And besides, I feel funny about taking advantage of such limited resources in a land with no refrigeration. I have no problem with the team sharing this gift of the road, but I can't myself. It's another moment of awareness that I'm going back home to a place where such a treat is so common as to be unremarkable. I can wait. On the other hand, if I had taken a cold bottle of water, I would not have thought that badly of myself.

One More District

I'M SURE THAT OUR tour is over. There's no more that I need to learn. Things are all repeating themselves. My mental energy is depleted, and I'm ready to pack it in. But Joseph Mulongo has one more district that has requested a visit. Nothing new here. There are more districts requesting visits than we can get to. At some point, we have to say, "No."

But Mulongo has already said yes, and I have to go with his plan. He has been right every time before. We'll have to take the boat; we can't get there by road. Actually, we could, but it's the long way around and through Mai-Mai-controlled country.

The next morning, we load the boat with our bicycles. Food and charcoal for the journey are packed into the bow. There are new faces on the boat, church leaders wanting to tag along and a few men and women hitching a ride back to their villages.

Of course, I have no idea where we're going, and I don't much care. My agenda is finished. This is a bonus boat ride into the unknown, so I'm enjoying the day on the river.

In a couple hours, we're pulling into Malemba-Nkulu, where we offload our cargo, mostly bags of grain that we transported as favors for friends. I don't know if we'll ever make money with this boat, what with carrying hitchhikers and doing favors for friends. No bother.

We drop passengers and pick up two pastors in Malemba who need rides home.

I love life on the river. Right now, as far as I'm concerned, Teri and I could spend retirement on a riverboat on the Congo, or pretty much any river, her choice, if she would agree to it. Today's trip takes us off the river into a network of canals through wetlands, into a large lake. The river is flat and slow through this region, resulting in plenty of marshlands and lakes. The canals connecting the lakes and the river are the country road version of the streets of Venice. The pirogue captain stands in the rear of his boat with a long paddle, not unlike the gondola's gondolier. There is an absolute beauty to this place that is so divorced from its poverty. On a day like today, I'm more in love with the beauty than I am concerned with the poverty, and I fear any attempt to save this land and its people that destroys its beauty. I'm not thinking of the landscape and wildlife so much as the pure beauty of life—people included, people foremost.

Éléphant goes forward to the forecastle with a long pole and punts our way through the marshes into a canal. How does he know the river and all its secret passages so well? From the looks of it, this could be a passage that leads to nowhere. We even come to some areas where the "trail" disappears, and there are arguments among the crew as to which direction we should take. As far as I know, we're lost in the tall grass of this swamp.

Eventually, the canal through the swamp opens up into a lake. This lake is large enough that we can't see the bank of the other side from here. Lily pads with purple and yellow flowers cover the place where we come out. I have my camera with the 200mm lens out, taking nature shots—hundreds of photographs of flowers and birds—dreaming of that perfect magazine cover photo. Every white crane gets a chance to be a star.

Back at the Yamaha outboard engine, Éléphant has to pick his way carefully through the field of lilies, stopping occasionally to clear the prop. He also has to watch for fishing lines and nets running just below the surface, marked by small bamboo floats.

It's a good hour or more across the lake to a bank where a river enters it. There's a fishing village on this bank, and it is a "bus" stop for boats like ours. We drop a passenger and pick one up. In fact, a boat our size is pulling out, headed for Malemba, loaded with people and bags of grain and fish. I'm thinking, if we can get this boat to pay for itself, we could buy two or three more to serve these remote districts, but we haven't broken the code yet on how to make this a moneymaker instead of a money pit. It's clear that the other boats do it by overloading and deferring maintenance.

We continue up the small river to Kayumba-Museka. The river narrows and becomes crowded with pirogue traffic: rush hour in Kayumba-Museka. An old man in his fishing pirogue tips his straw cowboy hat in a smiling welcome. The exchange feels genuine and level, with no hidden contempt for the white guy, no begging for a handout. He is a happy man. I try hard not to idealize or romanticize his life, but that man is content and happy to see me but too busy to stop what he's doing. A tip of the hat and a smile are sufficient welcome.

The riverbank that serves as the harbor is crowded with a small but odd armada of boats, most of which don't look seaworthy. There's even an old fiberglass runabout. I have to wonder how such a boat got here, like the shells of old Volkswagen Beetles we see upcountry. How did they get here?

A good-sized crowd with plenty of children underfoot has gathered on the bank to greet us. An old woman gets right up in my face shaking her finger at me and yelling something that cannot be a welcome. I'm simply told that she's a witch. Everyone chooses to ignore her, and eventually, she gives up and falls back into the crowd. She doesn't leave, though, and I can't get out of the sight of her evil eye. Women like this one are not rare. Every village has one. I once had a woman following me through a village calling me "Son of Mary." Better to be blessed than cursed, I guess.

The group walks just far enough up the bank to get clear of the river, and we park ourselves on chairs provided outside of some sort of community building.

It turns out I was wrong—the tour wasn't over, and I wasn't finished learning. This community building is something new. By the sign, I can figure out that it's some kind of homegrown NGO, a local development corporation, not one of the major chains (World Vision, UNICEF, USAID, GOAL), but rather a mom-and-pop concern. They're making concrete floor slabs for toilets. They're stacked out in the yard, concrete squares with the appropriate hole in the middle. I've been seeing these newly installed everywhere we've been this year. Last year, toilets had log or bamboo floors and just looked like disease-transmitting phone booths: "Enter here for cholera. Enter here for typhoid." The concrete floors for toilets are the best thing I've seen out here for combatting killer diseases. So many things are right with this picture—a local, community-created factory is manufacturing a simple solution to a major health problem.

There's more to learn. Last year we sent a young woman, Emily Johnson, a doctoral candidate at the University of Indianapolis, to Mulongo to get some field experience. She was brought here by Mary, who led a women's boat team. According to the local leadership, she was the first missionary to ever come to this village. That makes me the second. There has never been a resident missionary here. This community development runs on local initiative.

I'm impressed by the progress I see on our village tour.

There are two community wells, one at either end of the village, each with an operating pump and concrete floor. There is a sanitation project— a line of toilets at the primary school. And there is a small hospital, bigger than a clinic, funded by USAID, though I suspect no one from USAID has ever been here to see this.

Not only does this village have a locally created NGO, but they have also been good at recruiting grants from the big NGOs. How has this happened? Who is responsible? This is an almost inaccessible village that, on the surface, looks like so many other villages. How did it get all this development?

We get the answer when we meet the chief, our host.

Because we are in a remote village, we expect to be offered modest accommodations, or even to sleep in our own tents. But instead, we are taken to the chief's house. This is an exception. While we've always been welcomed by the chief in every village—if we had not been welcomed, we would not have stayed in the village—never before have we actually been invited to stay in the chief's home. In most villages, had we been invited to stay in the chief's home, it would not have been much different from staying with anyone else. Here, it is a major step up. There are poor chiefs, and there are rich chiefs. This is a rich chief.

His home is a grand house in a small village. The walled compound contains several outbuildings for depots and sleeping quarters for staff and a central paillotte for meetings and informal gatherings. The house itself is one story but has tall roofs and high ceilings for cooling. The exterior stucco is painted yellow and white.

Inside are tile floors and carved wood doors with hardware that appears to come from Dubai, where wealthy Africans often travel to purchase materials for their homes. The house is wired for electricity provided by a generator in the backyard.

The chief greets us in the foyer. We have been served Fantas.

He's about my age and commands the room in the way of Congolese chiefs. His dress is Congolese business casual. His English is only slightly better than my French, so our chat is a struggle.

He asks me if I know the missionaries Person. I say that I know David Person. But the chief means David's parents. He had been sent to the missionary school as a child and worked in the Persons' home. He talked about his ironing duties and learning math with David's mother. He credited the Persons with his education and his work habits.

This chief, a product of missionary schools, is now a chief-politician-businessman who is doing well for himself and is using his wealth and influence to leverage the good life for his village. Not everyone who attended a missionary school used their education well, but those who took advantage of their education and position had a tremendous head start. Of course, he had the advantage of being a chief's son and, eventually, a chief, but there are plenty of chiefs who are themselves suffering and provide little leadership for their villages.

In probably the most isolated village we are going to visit, we are treated to hotel-like accommodations. I feel a bit of relief after living off the hospitality of the very poor, and this is a reminder that it's getting to be time to go home.

Ashamed of the UMC

WE ARE SHOWN ONE building the people of this village are ashamed of—the United Methodist Church. It's falling down, and one wall has a crack running crookedly from bottom to top. What is the chief thinking when he, a United Methodist, a product of the missionary schools, gets funding for water wells, toilets, and a hospital, creates his own NGO, but refuses to fund the church? I wonder what the story might be.

There are several possibilities, the simplest being that he and the district superintendent don't get along. That's common. But this superintendent has a heart for development. It may be that the superintendent and the pastor don't get along. The superintendent may be blaming the pastor for the church's failing, and the chief is staying clear of the conflict. The chief may be a United Methodist in the general sense, but not so much a part of the local congregation. That's common, too. There are other possibilities. Maybe, it's just a matter of timing. They haven't gotten to it yet. But that raises the question of the order of community development and why rebuilding the church comes last in this village?

I note that we don't have worship here—that's a first.

One of the lessons we are learning is that not all churches are the same. Not all of them are the picture of enthusiastic worship we've come to expect. Some are struggling, and some are an embarrassment to the superintendent. I'm not saying that this one is such a case. I don't know. We aren't shown.

I remember being stuck in a village on a Saturday night when our Land Cruiser broke down on our way to Kabongo back in 2009. That Sunday morning, we dropped in on the United Methodist Church for worship to find an embarrassing crowd of nine, most of them the pastor's family. The excuse was that this was harvest time, and everyone was in the fields. That was probably true, but nine people? We got to drop in on a church when they weren't prepared to receive visitors.

The DS's School

THE DISTRICT SUPERINTENDENT WANTS us to see more of his district, so we get on our bikes and ride. If we followed this road out of town far enough, we would eventually connect with the Red Road, somewhere around Kyolo. That is how the chief gets his building supplies to Kayumba-Museka.

As we ride, the chief's fields of maize surround us. He owns all this farmland, and his fortune is in corn.

In an even smaller village about five kilometers down the road, we find a secondary school. The district superintendent is the director of this school. It may be more common than I know, but a district superintendent with a secondary appointment as the headmaster of a school seems unusual to me. He is proud of the school. Classes are not in session right now, but we get to meet one young man who is both a student and an assistant to the director.

Secondary schools typically have a themed curriculum. Some are auto mechanics, some electrical engineering, some agriculture. This one is development. The students here graduate with a major in community development. This is new. I'm beginning to get a picture of a district that focuses on development.

The day's ride takes us across several log bridges. I can see that getting a truck in here would be impossible during the rainy season and difficult, at best, during the dry season. We come to a river and have to cross by ferry. The ferry is a steel barge, just big enough for one truck. It has no motor and runs from one shore to another along a steel cable. It's an engineering marvel: the cable is run at a perfect angle to the current of the river, which is pretty strong. This arrangement allows the crew to tack the barge to be pushed by the current in either direction.

The crew is having fun with us. The bikes are loaded. As we cross, I'm wondering how many of these ferries are all over the rivers of Katanga.

We arrive at the village on the other end of this district. The chief is nice and friendly but obviously not as rich as our host in Kayumba-Museka. We are greeted in the church with a modified worship service of songs and greetings but no sermon. Lunch is served, and after that, we head back to Kayumba-Museka.

Truly Done

After the Kayumba-Museka visit, we are now truly done. It's a matter now of getting back to Lubumbashi. The Red Road is still held by the Mai-Mai militia and too dangerous for us to use. We'll have to go back around the way we came, by boat to Bukama, then by bicycle to Tenke.

Since we're running upstream, it's three days from Mulongo to Bukama by boat. Our earlier trip downstream from Bukama to Mulongo only took two days.

We stop for the first night at Kalombo, our familiar overnight campsite. The second night we are going to have to lay up in a village that we haven't stayed in before. It's tiny, right on the edge of the river, and flooded. Cholera city.

The approach through a mangrove is a cool experience. But that's where the cool part ends, and the scary begins. I'm thinking that I've completed three years of these tours, and now, at the end of this one, we're going into ground zero of a cholera epidemic. I do not fear malaria anymore. I have it all the time and can count on having a bout of it on these trips. But cholera scares me. It is irreversible and deadly. You get it, and the next day you're dead, and it's a painful death. This village is not where I want to be.

The first thing we need to do is set up the tents. We're not going to accept local hospitality. I don't have to say this; the whole team is on the same page. Instead: tents, on the only high ground we can find. Second, we have to visit the church. Protocol. The church is all grass, walls included. It is in standing water.

We also meet a regional community health worker here. I don't know where he came from or where he is going, but we run into all kinds of folk while traveling on the river. We listen to his concerns and commiserate with him. He understands the problem, he knows his job, but he is fighting a losing battle.

Now, I've got to get to a toilet. There is one, and it's one of those NGO-built toilets. However, it is on the other side of the flooded village, so I'll have to walk across a series of log bridges. I give it a try. This is not going to work. I don't have the required balance, and it's now dark.

At this point, I have lost all face in front of the village. The villagers come up with an alternative route. A pirogue is brought, and I cross the flood by dugout.

The toilet is built up on stilts. It's locked, and someone has brought the key. I can't see how this arrangement helps the village. One locked toilet dumping sewage into the flooded backwater. It's no secret why there is cholera here every rainy season.

In three years of traveling with my Congolese friends and colleagues, I have learned that there are essential, everyday skills they have developed that I just haven't:

First, they are accustomed to navigating in the dark, and I am not. I learned that on the bicycle and the many nights that we didn't get in before sunset.

Second, they can pick up a coal from the fire and move it around thanks to calluses built over years. I cannot. I learned that by watching them cook. They can also pick up a hot pan.

Third, they can walk on a single log to cross a cholera-infested pond or a raging river. I cannot.

It's time to go home.

My life runs in cycles. There is a time when I have to come here, and there is a time when I need to go home, to turn the page.

I'm going home.

Further Reading and Resources

To VIEW THE PHOTOGRAPHS taken by Bob on the journeys chronicled in this book, visit the United Methodist Church's General Commission on Archives and History digital library online at https://www.gcah.org

About the Tanenbaum Center Award: https://tanenbaum.org/blog/2010/11/celebrating-bishop-ntambo/

www.ingramcontent.com/pod-product-compliance
Lightning Source LLC
Chambersburg PA
CBHW051059160426
43193CB00010B/1241